CAPITAL FORMATION IN MAINLAND CHINA, 1952–1965

MICHIGAN STUDIES ON CHINA

*Published for the Center for Chinese Studies
of the University of Michigan*

MICHIGAN STUDIES ON CHINA

THE RESEARCH ON WHICH THIS BOOK IS BASED WAS
SUPPORTED BY THE CENTER FOR CHINESE STUDIES
AT THE UNIVERSITY OF MICHIGAN.

Capital Formation in Mainland China,

1952–1965

KANG CHAO

UNIVERSITY OF CALIFORNIA PRESS

BERKELEY, LOS ANGELES, LONDON

University of California Press
Berkeley and Los Angeles, California
University of California Press, Ltd.
London, England
Copyright © 1974, by
The Regents of the University of California
ISBN: 0–520–02304–8
Library of Congress Catalog Card Number: 72–85526
Printed in the United States of America

To Jessica, Tonia, and Constance

Contents

Tables

Appendix Tables

Acknowledgments

This study was originally prepared as part of a larger research project on the Chinese economy under the directorship of Professor Alexander Eckstein at the University of Michigan; it has been revised substantially. To Professor Eckstein and to two other colleagues, Professors Chu-yuan Cheng and Robert Dernberger, I am deeply grateful for their help in formulating the research methodology in the early stage of the study and for their reading and commenting on the draft in the final stage. I am equally grateful to those who read the draft and made valuable suggestions but chose to remain anonymous. I also wish to express my appreciation to the Center for Chinese Studies at the University of Michigan, whose financial support enabled me to carry out the research work embodied in this monograph. Needless to say, I am solely responsible for the opinions expressed here.

March 1973

                                                              Kang Chao

CHAPTER 1

Introduction

CHINA before the Communist era has often been considered a typical case of an overpopulated, underdeveloped economy trapped in a vicious circle of poverty and further impoverished by a series of wars. The low productivity of labor led to a low level of real income, which in turn meant a very thin margin of surplus for saving. A number of institutional factors and traditional misconceptions, such as the habit of hoarding gold and silver and the tendency to buy farmland as personal investment, prevented the meager savings from being channeled into capital formation. The slow capital formation meant a failure to raise productivity and per capita real income. So the vicious circle was complete.

Reliable information about China's economy has always been hard to come by. Before 1930, no serious attempt was made to study quantitatively capital formation in China. For the early 1930's, there are nine investment estimates compiled by economists.[1] These estimates differ in concept, estimation method, and valuation basis. What is more, they disagree with each other in magnitude over an enormous range. A recent study by Kung-chia Yeh provides some better estimates of investment in 1931–36. In that period, gross domestic capital formation ranged from 4.1 billion yuan to 6.1 billion yuan (in 1952 prices), or between 6.6 and 9 per cent of gross domestic product, with an average annual rate of investment of 7.5 per cent. Out of the total investment, the pro-

1. For a summary of the nine studies, see Kung-chia Yeh, *Capital Formation in Mainland China, 1931–36 and 1952–57* (Ph.D. dissertation, Columbia University, 1965), p. 109.

1

portion of investment in inventories varied from zero to 8.1 per-cent.[2] It should be noted that in spite of the endeavors made by the new government in Nanking to stimulate investment and in-dustrialization, large-scale military conflicts between the Nationalist and Communist troops were still going on. It is no surprise that the investment rate rose only slowly.

The low rate of investment generated in China's traditional economy left very little as net investment after worn-out capital goods were replaced. Yeh estimates capital consumption in 1931 at 3.15 billion yuan (in 1952 prices), or about 5 per cent of that year's GNP,[3] which seems a plausible figure. This is almost a mini-mum investment requirement even for a preindustrial economy with a nearly constant population, if the capital stock of the econ-omy is to be maintained at the same level. Only when the invest-ment exceeds that level would there be some net addition to the existing capital stock.

Our speculation is that net capital formation in China in 1931–36 probably was concentrated in modern manufacturing and min-ing industries located in a few big cities. According to one study, the rate of industrial growth in 1931–36 reached as high as 9.3 per cent per annum.[4] However, modern industry was too small a sector to influence substantially the level of per capita income in the whole country. Gross domestic product rose by only 1.6 per cent annually in this period; at the same time, according to a number of sample studies, the natural rate of increase of the Chinese popu-lation was about 1 per cent.[5] This means that the advance in per capita real income was only slightly better than a standstill.

When the Chinese Communists came to power in 1949, they certainly hoped to break the vicious circle. In fact, they wanted much more than that. One imperative objective of the new regime was to foster economic growth at a high speed. The approach that the Chinese Communist leaders adopted was essentially the strat-egy designed by Stalin for the Soviet Union in the 1930's, with only

2. K. C. Yeh, "Capital Formation," in *Economic Trends in Communist China*, ed. A. Eckstein, W. Galenson, and T. C. Liu, p. 511.

3. See Yeh, 1965 (n. 1 above), p. 73.

4. John K. Chang, *Industrial Development in Pre-Communist China* (Chicago, 1969), p. 71.

5. John L. Buck, *Land Utilization in China* (Nanking, 1937), pp. 383–387.

minor adaptations to Chinese conditions. In order to survive, the Soviet policy makers in the early years had to design a special model which could promise a high growth rate so that their relatively underdeveloped country could catch up with advanced capitalist countries in a fairly short period of time. Moreover, in view of the Soviet Union's probably prolonged isolation, the growth model must be built on the assumption of a closed economy, that is, foreign trade could not be depended upon.

The Chinese Communist leaders inherited the same spirit despite the different situation confronting them. They pledged to catch up with advanced capitalist countries in the shortest possible period of time. They also set as an ultimate goal the establishment of a "comprehensive and independent industrial system." In many ways the Chinese Communists sounded more ambitious and less patient than their Russian predecessors several decades earlier, perhaps because China had to begin industrialization from a more backward point.

One outstanding feature of Communist countries in pursuing economic growth is that they are able to minimize some barriers to domestic saving and mobilize a maximum amount of surpluses for economic construction. One cornerstone of the theory of the vicious circle of poverty is that capital formation is ordinarily constrained by peoples' propensity to save. However, in a system in which the state controls practically all means of production and sets prices and wages, private consumption is subject to the direct manipulation of the government. In other words, within a reasonably wide range the low propensity to save no longer forms a constraint because the government has ample power to mobilize compulsory savings.

In addition to capital formation, the Chinese Communists visualized another route for raising productivity; they intended to undertake both concurrently. For the nonagricultural sector, productivity and output were to be raised through the expansion of capital. For agriculture, however, the Communists hoped to promote productivity and output through institutional changes with a minimum amount of capital investment.[6] The designers of this

6. This is where the Chinese strategy differs from the Soviet strategy. The Soviet planners took agricultural collectivization as an extractive policy, whereas the Chinese Communists took it as a development policy.

policy were convinced that the Socialist transformation of the rural sector would enable the government to mobilize more inputs which were previously underutilized or unused. Moreover, it was believed that the existing inputs could be utilized more efficiently under the new institution of collective farming. Consequently, institutional changes could serve as a substitute for capital investment in the countryside. This would permit them to pour most of the investable funds controlled by the state into industry in order to attain a higher growth rate there.

In very broad terms, the Communist policy of concentrating as much investment as possible in industry is not too different from the distribution pattern of investment in the 1930's. But if one examines the detailed plan of allocating industrial investment, the different directions of emphasis in the two periods are clear. Judging from the types of modern factories that were established or expanding in the 1930's, industrial investment went preponderantly into light industry and consumer goods production such as cotton textiles, flour mills, and factories manufacturing cigarettes and matches. In contrast, the policy of the Chinese Communists, following the Stalin model, was to accord the highest priority to the production of producer goods.

While the guiding principles for economic development in China had been determined in the very beginning of the regime, the first detailed long-term plan was formulated and implemented only after three years of economic rehabilitation. Toward the end of the First Five-Year Plan period (1953–57), a number of new problems arose, requiring a thorough review of current economic policy. The leaders seem to have divided into two groups with different views on two major aspects of capital formation: the proper speed and the choice of priorities. While details of the debate are still not known to the outside world, indications are that one group was in favor of slowing down the pace of investment on the one hand and reducing somewhat the emphasis on producer goods production on the other. The second group, presumably led by Mao Tse-tung personally, insisted on maintaining the same order of priorities and wanted to accelerate further the tempo of capital formation.

Obviously, the latter group won the debate. The resulting policy of 1958, known as the Great Leap Forward, may be regarded as the pushing of the previous investment pattern to the extreme at a fantastic speed. A new feature, however, was introduced at the same time, namely the Walking with Two Legs movement—a planned industrial dualism. The chief idea was to obtain a greater output increase with a given amount of new investment by building numerous small plants using indigenous and labor-intensive methods of production.

This dangerous economic policy, when compounded by bad crops in three consecutive years and the worsening of the Sino-Soviet rift, brought the economy to the brink of collapse. In short, two types of imbalances in the economy were created by the investment policy. First, there were serious imbalances between industry and agriculture, which supplied food and raw materials to the former, and between consumer goods production and producer goods production within the industrial sector. Second, and perhaps more important, there existed an imbalance between investment and consumption. Since the high rate of investment was made possible only at the expense of increases in mass consumption, the incentives of the working people had been seriously hurt.

As the crisis deepened and Mao's influence subsided, the more pragmatic group in the Party ascended to power. Their corrective measures entailed, among other things, a drastic decrease in the tempo of capital formation in order to raise personal consumption. The priorities of development were also reversed to put agriculture first, followed by light industry and heavy industry.[7] This policy of "readjustment, consolidation, reinforcement, and improvement" lasted until 1965, when the economy was finally fully recovered.

In order to measure and assess these sharp changes in investment policy and performance between the pre-Communist and Communist eras and between different periods within the Communist era, it is necessary to calculate the relevant magnitudes in quantitative terms. Unfortunately, the investment statistics officially published by Peking cannot be used directly for this purpose. Instead, we must construct independent estimates in order to ascertain the rates, acceleration, deceleration, and changes in the distribution pattern of capital formation in Communist China from 1952 to 1965.

7. See Chou En-lai's speech before the National People's Congress on March 27, 1962, published in *JMJP*, April 17, 1962.

Our estimating procedures begin, in chapter 2, with an examination of the official investment statistics and previous estimates made by Western scholars, in order to discover what weaknesses the existing statistics contain and what improvements need to be made. We are then ready to construct our new estimates of fixed capital formation. Because of the disparity in quality and availability of basic data for the period 1952–57 and the period 1958–65, the two periods are treated separately, in chapters 3 and 4. These two chapters (and Appendix C) explain the methodology used and all statistical details. The reader who is not interested in scrutinizing our estimation methods but is primarily eager to know the results of the analyses may read only the summaries of chapters 3 and 4 before proceeding to the remaining analytical chapters.

The reader should be cautioned at the outset that the dearth of data leaves us with a weak estimation basis for the period 1958–65. Many gaps in information have to be bridged by rough approximations. Occasionally we can only resort to "educated guesses." In view of the uncertainties involved, we examine at some length the merits and demerits of possible alternative methods of estimating. Finally, we obtain two sets of estimates for this period. Toward the end of chapter 4, we compare the two sets and subject them to various tests in order to determine their relative credibility and to choose one for use in the subsequent analyses. Since we are not sure that our judgment is conclusive enough, however, we have presented both series to the reader.

In chapters 5, 6, and 7, we analyze various aspects of capital formation in the Communist era, topic by topic, as revealed by our new estimates of investment. As the reader will soon note, in spite of our best efforts the limited information for the years after 1958 prevents us from giving symmetrical treatments to the two periods.

In the final chapter, we summarize the results of our analysis and attempt to answer two questions: (1) Are the differences in investment levels between the pre-Communist and Communist eras and among different periods in the Communist era merely phases of long-term investment cycles, or are they related to changes in economic institutions? and (2) What role did capital formation play in economic growth during the period 1952–65?

CHAPTER 2

Chinese Official Data and
Independent Estimates
of Investment

DURING THE 1950's, the Peking government published data on investment rather regularly. The statistical blackout did not begin until 1960, when the regime found itself in a deep economic crisis. The quality of the published investment data is regarded by Western students of the Chinese economy as relatively good compared with other types of official economic statistics.

The reason for this relatively good rating of the investment statistics is that they are subject to less exaggeration by individual reporting units. Gross values of production, be they for industry or agriculture, are collected basically from individual production units which, under the prevailing incentive system, tend to embellish their performance in their statistical reports whenever possible. Investment data are compiled, however, through an entirely different channel. Since a preponderant portion of total investment is financed by the state budget in accordance with approved plans for construction projects, investment data are primarily based on actual government expenditures. With a generally well controlled government accounting system and the rigid supervision over investment outlays by the People's Construction Bank and its branches, it would be difficult for government agencies to fabricate investment expenditures.

Nor do government agencies or construction units have any mo-

7

tivation to inflate investment figures in value terms, given the incentive structure prevailing in most of the years under the Communist regime. For industrial firms, there is a strong inducement to overreport, whenever possible, their production figures, since failure to meet production targets is penalized and exceeding the assigned targets is rewarded. However, the incentive structure for the investment and construction units is different. To overspend on an investment project would invite certain penalties; to spend less than the investment budget would bring rewards. Therefore, there is no enticement for construction units or investing units to inflate their investment figures.

True, there have been reports that construction units occasionally attempted to exaggerate their accomplishments by including equipment in storage as installed equipment or by overstating the volume of work in progress.[1] Tricks like these would distort the time distribution of a given amount of investment but not the total volume of investment. The installation work of a construction firm is exaggerated for the current period if equipment in storage has been reported as equipment installed in this period; but the firm's work volume would be understated in the next period, when this piece of equipment is actually installed. The total investment for that project would be left intact. In other words, although this scheme may save a construction firm from a temporary failure to meet assigned targets, it would not enable the firm to report some installation work when there was nothing to be installed, nor to install something which the firm has not been authorized to buy and to install.

However, the fact that official investment data are relatively free of deliberate fabrication does not necessarily mean that they are immediately usable. In fact, there is a great hazard in directly using official investment data for analytical purposes. The difficulties fall into two groups. First, the official investment data are divided into too many categories, and these categories not only differ in coverage but also depart, in some cases, from Western concepts of investment. The reader may easily be confused by the various headings, and without careful scrutiny he cannot tell precisely how

1. CSYK, 1957, No. 7, p. 30; TCKT, 1958, No. 2, p. 12; and HHYP, 1955, No. 10, p. 173. A list of abbreviations for Chinese publications is given in the bibliography.

those indicators differ from each other. In addition, since many of the terms are defined in peculiar ways and contain some elements which should not be called investment in the conventional sense, they are not readily comparable with investment data of other countries, particularly non-Communist countries. Second, even after the definitional confusion is eliminated, there still exist several complicating factors which may distort investment magnitudes.

In the following sections, we shall first examine these two problems with the official investment data and then discuss the problems with several independent estimates which have been made by Western scholars.

1. OFFICIAL DEFINITIONS AND CLASSIFICATIONS OF INVESTMENT COMPONENTS

A number of terms such as "basic construction," "new fixed assets," and "accumulation" are commonly used in Chinese publications to indicate the magnitude or scale of investment. These designations are closely related, but not identical, to each other. They are usually further differentiated by references to "within state plans" and "within and outside state plans." Detailed definitions and explanations are given in Appendix A; the relationships of these terms can be roughly summarized here as follows:

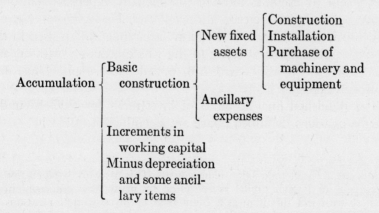

The term "new fixed assets" is roughly equivalent to the Western concept of gross investment in physical capital. "Basic construction" is broader in coverage because it includes many items of ancillary expenses. The ancillary items are conventionally not considered as investment components in the West.[2] Both new fixed assets and basic construction are gross in concept, namely, inclusive of depreciation. The two categories are further differentiated according to whether the investment projects fall under the state plans and whether the funds are drawn from government budgets.

Moreover, a distinction is made between "basic construction investment" and the "volume of basic construction completed." The former embraces all investment work done in place, whereas the latter term refers to the completed portion. Specifically, when the whole construction project is completed, it is called a "completed project." For a large project, when an independent unit is finished before the completion of the whole project, this portion is called "finished work" on an "unfinished project." Of course, there is "unfinished work" on an "unfinished project." While all three categories are included in "basic construction investment," only the first two categories are counted in the "volume of basic construction completed." The two magnitudes would become equal only when the volume of "unfinished work" has remained the same at the beginning and at the end of the year.

The term "accumulation" has the broadest coverage among all designations used in Communist China to measure investment activities. It is very close to the Western concept of net domestic investment. It excludes most of the ancillary expenses mentioned above but includes increases in inventories. Furthermore, it is net of depreciation. Whenever the term "accumulation" is used in the Chinese publications, it refers to the whole economy without any breakdown of quantities within or outside state plans. Thus, it is always an aggregate figure.

The published final accounts of investment for 1952–57 under the designations described above are assembled in table 1.

2. Interestingly, one of the ancillary items is the expense of training technicians to meet production requirements. This fits well the definition of investment in human capital as suggested by many Western economists. Even so we reject this item as a component of investment, for reasons of international comparability (the Western countries do not include human capital in their national income accounts) and consistency (the Chinese Communist practice fails to count many other items of investment in human capital as investment).

Table 1

OFFICIAL DATA ON INVESTMENT UNDER DIFFERENT DESIGNATIONS,
1952–57

(in millions of yuan)

	1952	*1953*	*1954*	*1955*	*1956*	*1957*
Accumulation, at current prices	11,440	16,071	17,333	17,390	20,905	19,839
Accumulation, at 1952 prices	11,440	16,037	17,375	18,177	23,010	22,171
Basic construction, within the state plan, at current prices	3,710	6,510	7,500	8,630	13,990	12,640
Basic construction, outside the state plan, at current prices	650	1,490	1,570	670	810	1,190
Basic construction, within and outside the state plan, at current prices	4,360	8,000	9,070	9,300	14,800	13,830
New fixed assets, within the state plan, at current prices	3,110	6,560	7,370	8,020	11,160	12,920

SOURCE: Compiled by Nai-ruenn Chen, *Chinese Economic Statistics: A Handbook for Mainland China*, pp. 141, 145, 158, and 163.

2. POSSIBLE DISTORTIONS IN
OFFICIAL INVESTMENT DATA

Aside from the difficulties we have described with the official definitions, there are also possibilities that official investment data may have been distorted from what they profess to show. The distortion may stem from two sources: (1) the incomplete or changing coverage of investment magnitudes under certain designations, and (2) the use of unreasonable valuation bases.

One example of incomplete and changing coverage is that prior to 1956 anything worth more than 500 yuan and having a normal life span of more than one year was classified as a fixed asset. Thus, many small items that are ordinarily regarded as fixed assets had actually been excluded from the Chinese statistics on fixed investment. This value limit was lowered from 500 yuan to 200 yuan in 1956. By virtue of this definitional change, the coverage of "new fixed assets" and "basic construction" was enlarged. Consequently, an upward bias was introduced in the rates of increase in fixed investment. In other words, Chinese official data on basic construction and new fixed assets for the years before 1956 are not comparable with those for the years since 1956.

Another example is the fact that the scope of the state investment plan was widened in 1957 to include some basic construction activities that were previously classified as investment outside the state plan. Although this change did not alter the coverage of overall investment, it enabled the government to show unduly high rates of increase in investment within the state plan after that year.

A more serious distortion is found in the magnitudes of basic construction investment outside the state plan. As can be seen from table 1, the amounts of basic construction outside the state plan in various years appear to be not commensurate with the indicated coverage. The amounts are too large for the investment made by labor unions, joint enterprises, and state enterprises with their own funds, but too small if we include investment activities of private firms, agricultural cooperatives, and individual farmers.

One possible explanation may be that since only investment items above 200 or 500 yuan in value were counted, a large portion of private investment was automatically excluded from the official calculation. This omission has an especially serious effect on the quantity of private investment in the rural sector, because most of the investments of individual farmers and cooperatives are in farm implements and other small assets with unit values below the 200 yuan or 500 yuan limit. Even some rural housing construction falls short of that limit. This explanation seems to be supported by a comparison of official data on basic construction investment for "agriculture, forestry, water conservation, and meteorology." The total amount of basic construction investment for this category within and outside the state plan for the whole period 1953–57 is officially given as 4,190 million yuan,[3] whereas that within the state

3. TGY, p. 57.

plan for the same period is 3,864 million yuan.[4] The difference between the two is 326 million yuan, or 65 million yuan per annum. This quantity is obviously far too small to account for the total gross private fixed investment during that period for the vast rural sector in China.

Now, let us turn to the second type of possible distortion in official investment data, namely, the problems stemming from the valuation bases used by the Chinese statistical authorities in computing investment.

The truly ideal valuation basis should satisfy a fundamental principle: the prices which are the coefficients or weights generally used to value quanta should be scarcity prices, so that the calculated amount of investment in any given period of time can reflect faithfully the real opportunity costs of investment for the economy as a whole. This principle is violated in Communist China, because prices are not determined in a competitive market.

The aforementioned problem exists in virtually all Communist countries. However, the Chinese Communist valuation basis has other peculiarities which are unique to that country and which have caused further distortions in the official investment data. For meaningful valuation, price weights, however determined, should be applied consistently: two identical items should be assigned the same value if they appear in the same period or point of time. This principle has been clearly violated in Communist China in two major cases.

The first case involves the valuation of construction projects using, partially or entirely, corvée labor, otherwise known as draft labor or work brigades. One special feature of construction in Communist China is the extensive employment of draft labor. It is made up mainly of peasants mobilized from the neighborhoods of construction sites. A small portion of draft labor consists of prisoners in the "labor reform camps"[5] and students, teachers, and government employees, who "volunteer" to work on nearby construction projects.[6] The total amount of draft labor was estimated at 498 million man-days in 1952 and 3,519 million man-days in

4. *CHCC*, 1958, No. 2, p. 17.
5. *CHCC*, 1958, No. 4, p. 27.
6. *KMJP*, June 23, 1952, and *CKCNP*, Nov. 2, 1954.

1958.[7] Those mobilized peasants and other draft laborers are usually sent to work on large water conservation projects and highway and railway construction.

In return for their work, draft laborers are provided meals and perhaps shelter if the construction sites are too far from their homes. Sometimes draft laborers receive cash payments instead, which are barely enough to buy food to keep them alive. They are underpaid in the sense that if a regular worker were hired to perform the same task, he would receive a much higher wage. In valuing a construction project involving draft labor, the government calculates all the work done by draft labor at the actual cost, that is the actual expenditures on meals, shelter, or the cash compensations.[8]

One may attempt to justify this statistical practice by identifying draft labor with disguised unemployment in the rural sector and by arguing that draft labor really commands no opportunity cost. This argument, however, is objectionable on several grounds. First, this statistical practice obviously contradicts the consistency principle. Earth work on housing projects and on other small-scale civil engineering projects has been performed by regular construction workers who are paid at standard rates, whereas draft labor doing the same kind of earth work is paid less. Why should two units of work identical in physical terms, for example, same amount of cubic meters of dirt removed, be worth two drastically different values simply because they have been undertaken by two different groups of wokers? Second, judging by the total amount of draft labor employed by the government each year and in view of some information revealing the actual labor supply in the rural sector during the period under study, we can hardly conclude that those mobilized peasants would have been otherwise left idle in the countryside. Not all of them represent disguised unemployment, and their working on construction projects does involve some opportunity costs. Perhaps a more realistic view is to treat corvée labor as a sort of tax paid in kind by peasants. The tax in kind should be valued in full, and the imputed revenue which is spent on construction projects should be recorded.

The second case of inconsistent valuation is found in the treat-

7. Kang Chao, *The Construction Industry in Communist China,* table A-7.
8. *TCKT,* 1957, No. 1, p. 12.

ment of imported goods. As will be shown later, a great deal of machinery and equipment installed in China in the 1950's came from abroad. Therefore, an unreasonable pricing practice for imported capital goods could seriously distort the magnitude of total annual investment. Specifically, when there are two identical pieces of machinery, one domestically produced and the other one imported, the value or prices of these to the final users in the country should be the same. This is easily attained, in a general sense, in a free market economy. In such an economy, if the price of an imported machine to the final user is higher than that of a domestically produced piece with exactly the same quality and specifications, importation of that machine will be curtailed, through the interplay of supply and demand forces, until the two prices become equal. However, this is not the case in Communist China. Chinese official publications have disclosed that (1) domestically produced machines and almost identical sets imported from abroad usually have drastically different prices to the users, and (2) the same kinds of machines imported from different countries usually have different prices.

These phenomena result from the pricing practice for imported goods and the peculiar exchange rate system. One Chinese Communist source has described their practice of pricing imported goods as follows: "There are two ways of determining the transfer prices of import commodities. (1) Prices of import commodities which are to be turned over to commercial departments or have been bought with the foreign exchange provided by local governments are determined according to domestic price levels. (2) For other departments or units which have ordered import commodities, the transfer prices are basically set at the importation costs plus three percent service fee." [9] Virtually all capital goods (machinery and equipment) imported by China go through the second channel. Thus, their transfer prices are independent of domestic price levels and depend on the actual importation costs in yuan terms. The problem is then to examine the reasonableness of the exchange rates used to calculate their importation costs.

The exchange rate system used by the Chinese government is indeed peculiar. It is recognized that, in a centrally planned economy like China's, official exchange rates have very little economic

9. *CHCC*, 1958, No. 4, p. 28.

meaning except as conversion rates between foreign and local currencies. But, since conversion rates still have an accounting function, unreasonable exchange rates definitely have some distorting effects on cost accounting. Whenever imported capital goods are used, investment data are distorted.

The exchange rate system of Communist China has been extremely complex not only because it has been a multiple-rate system but also because the exchange rates between yuan and various foreign currencies have been inconsistent in relation to each other. The yuan-ruble rates have been especially confusing. While detailed explanations about the history of the yuan-ruble rates are given in Appendix B, their features relevant to the study of capital formation are discussed briefly here. The Chinese currency unit, yuan (jen min pi), in the following exchange rates refers to the unit after the 1955 monetary reform. The old yuan prior to the monetary reform has been converted into the new yuan at the rate of 10,000 to 1.

TRADE RATES

Rate	Effective Period
0.95 yuan to the ruble	from April 1950 to December 31, 1959
0.80 yuan to the ruble	from unknown date to December 31, 1959
0.50 yuan to the ruble	from January 1, 1960, to December 31, 1960
2.22 yuan to the new ruble	since January 1, 1961

NONTRADE RATES

Rate	Effective Period
0.6754 yuan to the ruble	from June 1, 1951, to September 22, 1953
0.50 yuan to the ruble	from September 23, 1953, to December 31, 1959
0.1667 yuan to the ruble	from January 1, 1958, to December 31, 1960
1.667 yuan to the new ruble	from January 1, 1961, to March 31, 1963
1.29 yuan to the new ruble	since April 1, 1961

The following features must be noted. First, before January 1, 1958, there existed two trade rates and one nontrade rate between the yuan and the ruble. In the period between January 1, 1958, and December 31, 1959, there were two trade rates and two nontrade rates. It was only after December 31, 1959, that the system was simplified to a single trade rate and a single nontrade rate. Second, as will be shown later, none of these ruble-yuan rates was consistent with the yuan-dollar rate and the ruble-dollar rate.

Third, the whole matter is further complicated by the fact that transactions in ordinary Sino-Soviet trade have been priced and recorded first in rubles and then converted into yuan in the Chinese bookkeeping of foreign trade by using the trade ruble rates, whereas the transactions of trade financed by the Soviet loans to China have been recorded in a different way.[10] Some Soviet loans were stated in American dollars, some loans directly in yuan, and still other loans in rubles. However, for all transactions financed by Soviet credits, the trade ruble-yuan rates were not used; instead, a conversion rate was derived from the prevailing ruble-dollar and yuan-dollar rates.[11] As already noted, the cross rate so derived was not identical to any existing trade rate between the ruble and the yuan. Consequently, the special accounting procedure for credit-financed trade with the Soviet Union amounts to adding another trade exchange rate distinctly different from those listed above. The shipments from the Soviet Union to China financed by the Soviet credits were on the "Commodity List C," to be distinguished from ordinary imports from the Soviet Union, which were on the "Commodity List A." China could not use the Soviet credits to cover any deficits in current ordinary trade between the two countries. The actual sum of the Soviet loans received by China in a year was the total value of goods on the "C" list actually delivered to China in that year. The undelivered balance was to be treated as a remainder to be carried over to the next year.[12]

10. See Kang Chao, "Pitfalls in the Use of China's Foreign Trade Statistics," *China Quarterly*, July–September 1964, pp. 55–60; and Iu. V. Vladimirov, "The Question of Soviet-Chinese Economic Relations in 1950–1966," translated in *Chinese Economic Studies* 3, no. 1 (1969).

11. See Vladimirov, *op. cit.* He explicitly states that even when the Soviet credits were originally expressed in rubles, they were then converted into dollars at the exchange rate of 4 rubles to the dollar.

12. See Kang Chao, "Pitfalls," p. 56.

Trade between China and Communist countries other than the Soviet Union is carried out with the trade ruble as the accounting unit. In fact, except for Rumania, China has had nontrade exchange rates but no trade rates between the Chinese yuan and the currencies of those Communist countries. Therefore, the official values of China's trade with other Communist countries are subject to the same distortions.

The exchange rates between the Chinese yuan and currencies of non-Communist countries have been less complicated than the rate between the yuan and the ruble. Prior to 1957, there were two rates between the yuan and a non-Communist currency. One rate was called the "clearing rate," applicable to trade transactions only, while the other was the nontrade rate. Beginning in 1957, all nontrade rates for non-Communist currencies were abolished and the clearing rates were applied to both types of transactions.[13] However, the clearing rates themselves have been adjusted several times. As an example, the clearing rate for the dollar has been as follows:

1950–Dec. 1952	2.2–4.2 yuan to the dollar
Dec. 1952–1953	2.46 yuan to the dollar
1954–mid-1957	2.36 yuan to the dollar
mid-1957–1972	2.617 yuan to the dollar

It is now quite clear that the yuan-dollar and yuan-ruble rates have been inconsistent in the sense that no matter which pair of yuan-dollar and yuan-ruble rates one takes, a cross rate exactly equal to the official ruble-dollar rate, which was 4:1 before 1961 and 0.90:1 after 1961, cannot be derived. In the time period before 1961, the inconsistent exchange rate system overvalued the yuan in relation to the dollar but undervalued the yuan in relation to the ruble.[14]

The result of this inconsistency in the exchange rate system, combined with the separation of the prices of imported commodities from domestic prices, was differences in valuation bases (1)

13. *FKHP*, 1957, p. 59, articles 1 and 6.
14. For a detailed explanation on this point, see Kang Chao, "Pitfalls," and Alexander Eckstein, *Communist China's Economic Growth and Foreign Trade*, Appendix C.

between imported and domestically produced capital goods and (2) between capital goods imported from different countries.

For example, according to a Chinese official handbook for designing and budgeting construction projects, the prices of thirty-one Soviet machines exclusive of transportation costs, when converted into yuan, are 41.5 per cent higher than domestic prices of the same machines; and the prices of fifty-one machines imported from Eastern Germany and Czechoslovakia are 57.9 per cent higher.[15] According to another article, when the Anshan Steel Mill began its reconstruction work it bought two sets of furnaces from abroad. The total cost for each set was 6.32 million yuan. Later on Anshan added three more sets of furnaces, which had generally the same specifications and capacities as the first two sets but were manufactured in China with the technical assistance of Russian experts. The total cost for each set produced at home was only 3.7 million yuan (the price ratio is then 171:100). The prices of coking furnaces of the same specifications and capacities were 3.74 million yuan for imported ones and 1.43 million yuan for domestic products (the price ratio is 262:100). The same article further points out that for principal equipment used in mining, steel-making, and steel-rolling, prices of domestic products were lower than those of imports by one-third to one-half (implying a price ratio ranging from 150:100 to 200:100). For some machines, the price differentials were as large as three times.[16]

Up to 1960 the overvaluation of machinery and equipment imported from the Communist countries was offset by the undervaluation of those from the Western countries only to a very small extent, because in that period a much smaller quantity of capital goods was imported from the West than from the Communist countries.

3. FLAWS IN PREVIOUS INDEPENDENT WESTERN ESTIMATES

The reasons for rejecting the official investment data, and the need to construct independent estimates, are clear. There are two possible ways to derive new estimates. One way is to use basically the

15. *JPRS*, 10913, Oct. 31, 1961, pp. 24–26.
16. *JMJP*, June 5, 1957.

official aggregate investment data but adjust them for conceptual differences and valuation problems. If the official data on basic construction are to be used as the basis for estimating gross fixed capital investment, the following adjustments are required:

Adjustments for coverage:
1. Eliminate the noninvestment elements in official data, such as ancillary expenses and costs of purchasing existing assets
2. Add major repairs
3. Add the investment not covered by official data
4. Adjust for the changed coverage of official data, such as the changed value limit of "new assets"

Adjustments for valuation problems:
5. Deflate the official data which are given in current prices
6. Adjust the undervalued draft labor
7. Adjust the values of imports of machinery and equipment distorted by the official exchange rates

After all the adjustments have been made, the results may be added to estimated working capital investments to arrive at total gross investment. Official data on basic construction are readily available for the 1950's, but some adjustments listed above are difficult to do.

Four major sets of estimates made by Western scholars have made use of this approach, i.e. to begin with the official data on basic construction and then make adjustments. However, they differ considerably in the number, method, and degree of sophistication of the adjustments they have made. Space does not permit a detailed criticism and analysis of their methods. Here we shall only point out which of the seven necessary adjustments listed above have been attempted in each of the four sets of estimates:

TYPES OF ADJUSTMENTS

	(1)	(2)	(3)	(4)	(5)	(6)	(7)
Liu-Yeh, I	yes	yes	yes	no	yes	yes	no
Liu-Yeh, II	yes	yes	yes	no	yes	yes	no
Yeh	yes	yes	yes	no	yes	yes	no
Hollister	no	yes	yes	no	no	no	no

The second approach to deriving new investment estimates is to discard official aggregate statistics on investment, except as a reference point or a comparison basis, and to begin with individual components of investment. In this case, there is no need for coverage adjustments because we include only those items which should be included. Whenever valuation distortions appear in some individual component series, adjustments can be made to eliminate them. However, this approach, sometimes referred to as the commodity flow method, calls for more detailed statistics.

One Western scholar, C. M. Li, has used the commodity flow approach. Li has incorporated four components in his estimate of fixed capital investment:

1. State investment in machinery and equipment
2. State investment in construction other than housing
3. State investment in housing
4. Private and collective investment in agriculture[17]

However, owing to the lack of detailed statistics, his computation is crude, and we believe that the coverage of his estimate is incomplete. Moreover, the Li estimate differs from other sets in that it is net of depreciation.

In our study we have decided to use the commodity flow approach. Because of deficiencies in data we will confine ourselves to the estimation of fixed capital formation only, i.e. exclusive of inventory increases. Furthermore, we exclude military durables[18] and consumer durables other than residential housing. In other words, we intend to measure annual increases, over a specified period, of all capital goods in the hands of producers, private and public, and government offices and institutions, plus all residential construction.

Essentially, we try to estimate the users' costs of construction and installation, machinery and equipment produced and imported, office furniture and tools, and other rural investment. For any year, these components of fixed capital goods are combined to make the

17. C. M. Li, *Economic Development of Communist China*, p. 136.
18. That is, military hardware such as weapons, military aircraft, and naval vessels, which are usually treated as inventories. Investment in factories designed to produce military goods is included in our measurement.

aggregate investment in the economy. The aggregate investment figures so derived are gross of depreciation and major repairs.

Our estimates are in constant prices. Whenever possible 1952 prices are used as the evaluation bases. It is fully recognized that even the 1952 prices in Communist China were not scarcity prices in the strict sense. Other objections may be raised if the weights of an early year are used as the only weighting system when the study covers a long period of time. Unfortunately, the choice of prices is largely dictated by data availability, which does not leave us too much freedom.

Data availability also determines the degree of statistical refinement in our estimation processes for different time periods. Our detailed estimation methods vary considerably between the period 1952–57 and the period 1958–65. The estimates for the years after 1958 must be rather crude, pending further information.

CHAPTER 3

Estimation of
Fixed Capital Formation
in 1952–57

O UR ESTIMATE of the aggregate investment in fixed capital in the period 1952–57 is derived by combining the following component series: (1) construction and installation, (2) domestic production of machinery and equipment, (3) net imports of machinery and equipment, (4) office furniture and tools, and (5) other rural investment. Since conceptually we should value capital goods at the cost to their ultimate users, we must compute transportation costs and distribution margins and add them to the values of the component series. Only the highlights and important conceptual problems in the computation of each series will be discussed in this chapter; statistical details are left to the Appendix.

1. CONSTRUCTION AND INSTALLATION

In a previous study, we measured the output growth of the construction sector in China in the period 1950–58.[1] In addition to an adjusted official value index, we computed two independent indexes: an output-component index, based on fifteen important construction items, and an input index. A careful examination led to the conclusion that the input index is more satisfactory statistically

1. Kang Chao, *The Construction Industry in Communist China.*

than the output-component index. Therefore the input index of construction (see Appendix table A-1) will be used here as the basis for estimating the value of the construction component of fixed investment.

The input index, which was designed to measure the growth of all new construction and installation work at its real costs, was computed on the basis of the following items: construction steel, timber for construction, cement, glass plates, other building materials, regular construction workers, and work brigades. These items were weighted by their 1952 prices. The coverage of the index is much wider than it might at first appear to be, because "other building materials" is a catchall item for all products, other than cement and glass plates, produced by the building materials industry. The items we were not able to include in our calculation are capital inputs; the work performed by civil engineers, designers, and other staff members; overhead costs in construction enterprises; secondhand building materials; and indigenous building materials locally collected by farmers for their own housing construction.

This index serves here as an indicator of growth of the construction and installation component in fixed investment. The index will be converted into value terms to represent the total value of construction and installation works, at constant prices, for the country as a whole in each year of the period.

The total output value of the construction sector in 1952 is officially given as 4,560 million yuan.[2] This figure has a comprehensive coverage, namely, the value of all new construction and installation work done in the whole country in that year, including replacement of old houses and structures and all repair work. Unlike other Communist official measures of gross value of production, the gross output value of construction involves no double counting within that sector, because construction is a truly final stage of production; that is, no construction project is an intermediate good.

Besides the margins of statistical error that may have occurred in the process of compiling and estimating construction statistics, there is only one conceptual shortcoming discernible in the con-

2. *HH*, 1957, No. 2, pp. 24–26.

struction output figure. In the valuation of work done by draft labor, the authorities counted only the actual costs incurred by the government. As we noted in chapter 2, this accounting practice undervalues work done by draft labor because corvée workers are underpaid. We have estimated the total underpayment for corvée workers mobilized to do construction jobs in 1952 at 229 million yuan.[3] In order to remedy this conceptual defect, we add 229 million yuan to the original figure of 4,560 million yuan. The adjusted figure, 4,789 million yuan, is then used to convert our construction index numbers for 1953–57 (last column of table A-1) into value amounts, that is, to multiply 4,789 million yuan by each index number. Since construction projects are done on their sites, their total values are the costs to ultimate users. Following are the results (in millions of yuan):

1952	4,789	1955	10,062
1953	9,401	1956	15,622
1954	7,385	1957	13,989

2. DOMESTIC PRODUCTION OF MACHINERY AND EQUIPMENT

An index of domestic production of machinery and equipment for the period 1952–57 is independently computed from eighteen items of output series of machinery and their 1952 prices. Although military durables such as weapons, military aircraft, and naval ships are omitted in our calculation, machinery and equipment installed for the purpose of producing military goods are automatically included. For instance, many metal-cutting machine tools produced each year were installed for the armament industries, and a number of new spindles and looms were used to manufacture military uniforms and blankets.

The official data on physical output of machinery and equipment are published in such broad categories that sometimes an item can be used for both consumption and production purposes. Without sufficient information, we can hardly estimate the proportions of output of such an item for the two uses. For those

3. Kang Chao, *The Construction Industry in Communist China*, p. 216.

borderline cases, we have to make arbitrary decisions about whether they are preponderantly for production or consumption purposes. Thus, sewing machines, radios, and clocks are treated exclusively as consumer durables, whereas bicycles are regarded as means of local transportation.

Items like ball bearings are excluded because they are intermediate goods. To include them would lead to double counting.

As we did in the case of construction, we first develop an index of domestic production of machinery and equipment (see Appendix table A-2) as an indicator of growth and then convert the index into values. The total output value of the machine-building industry in 1952 is officially given as 1,400 million yuan; C. Y. Cheng has estimated that 59 per cent, or 826 million yuan, of this is the output value for nonmilitary goods.[4] However, this gross output value does contain slight double counting, for some machine-building factories produced parts and accessories to be used to make whole sets of machines or kept as spare parts for future repairs or maintenance. The degree of double counting depends on the statistical treatment of machine parts and intermediate goods. According to the "factory reporting method" used in Communist China, if the parts have been used or are to be used by the same factory that produced them, their value is not included in the gross output value of the factory. In other words, only the final products of a factory are included in the calculation of gross output value. However, if a factory specializes in parts production and supplies them to other factories, the value of the parts is fully counted as the gross value of output of that factory. Although there are no concrete statistics, very few factories in the period 1952–57 can be identified as specializing in production of machine parts and accessories. Most of them were factories producing ball bearings.

Civilian goods produced by the machine-building industry also include consumer durables. The important items are clocks, radios, and sewing machines. The total value of these three items plus ball bearings produced in 1952 has been estimated to be about 43 million yuan.[5] We raise this amount to 50 million yuan to take

4. Chu-yuan Cheng, *The Machine-Building Industry in Mainland China*, chap. 6.
5. *Ibid.*

into account other unidentifiable consumer durables and parts production. This figure is then subtracted from 826 million yuan to obtain the total output value of civilian machinery and equipment in 1952, exclusive of parts production and consumer durables. The resulting value, 776 million yuan, does not include the costs of transportation.

The next step, then, is to estimate transportation costs and distribution expenses in order to arrive at the costs to the final users of domestically produced machinery and equipment. According to one official investment budgeting handbook, transportation expenses for acquiring machinery and equipment are calculated from the rate schedule given in table 2. Apparently, the rates are not the

Table 2

RATES OF TRANSPORTATION EXPENSES FOR SHIPMENTS
OF MACHINERY AND EQUIPMENT
(percentage of original prices)

Region	Origin	
	Domestic	Foreign
Northeast China	2.5	12.5
North China, Inner Mongolia, East China	3.0	13.0
Central-South China	4.0	14.0
Southwest China, Kwangtung, Fukien	5.0	14.0
Yunan, Kweichow, Kansu	6.0	14.5

SOURCE: *Tieh-lu piao-chun she-chi yu-suan shou-tse* (Standard Railway Design and Budget Handbook), Peking: People's Railway Publishing Company, 1960; translated in *JPRS*, 10913, Oct. 31, 1961, p. 7.

actual freight charges but rather are estimated averages, based on past experience with transportation costs, created to assist planners in drawing up investment budgets. The transportation rates for machinery and equipment of domestic origin (the rates for imported goods will be discussed in the next section) are differentiated by the location of the final users. This practice has been used perhaps because of the fact that machine-building enterprises were heavily concentrated in Shanghai and Liaoning during that period of time[6] and the fact that the first three regions had better transportation with lower costs per ton-kilometer. Unfortunately, we have no information about the geographic distribution of the users of domestically produced machinery and equipment. We have arbitrarily set a national average transportation rate for domestically produced machinery and equipment at 3.5 per cent of their original prices.[7] This is lower than the median rate that can be calculated from the table, because we think that a relatively large proportion of users in that period were located in the first three regions.

During this period construction projects were carried out throughout the country, even in the remote provinces. As a result, the average transportation costs for building materials rose year after year. For instance, one official source indicates that the average haul of all building materials increased by 70 per cent during the period 1953–56.[8] This must also have been the case with transportation costs for new machinery and equipment. Therefore, to apply a flat rate of 3.5 per cent to all years may overstate the actual transportation costs in the early years. However, there is no statistical information enabling us to adjust for this.

We have added no distribution margin because most capital goods were directly allocated by the state to users who were state enterprises and government-financed construction projects. A "conference on purchase contracts," in which representatives of producers and users of capital goods got together, was held every year. Based on the state's allocation plan for the ensuing year, contracts

6. The geographic distribution of machinery production in 1955 is given (*CH*, p. 138) as follows (in percentage of total gross value of machine-building industry):

INLAND: 24.2
COASTAL AREAS: 75.8

Peking	3.2
Tientsing	7.2
Shanghai	25.4
Liaoning	27.4
Shantung	5.5

7. One Chinese source mentions that the average shipping cost plus other related expenses in purchasing domestically produced machinery and equipment was about 40 yuan per thousand yuan of commodity cost. See *JMJP*, June 7, 1957.

8. *CCTLKY*, 1958, No. 3, p. 15.

were signed between individual suppliers and buyers, determining detailed quantities and specifications of the goods and delivery dates. No wholesale channels or other distribution agencies were involved. It is true that a certain amount of machinery and equipment did go through wholesale markets and was eventually sold, for instance, to peasants and agricultural cooperatives, but the percentage is too small (about 10 per cent) to cause an appreciable bias in our calculation.

Two more points must be clarified. First, what we have computed are the values of current production in various years. In a given year, the machines produced may not equal the machines installed, either because some of them are for inventories or because there is a time lag between production and installation. No remedy can be devised for this matter. Some margin of error may have arisen from this source, unless inventory changes in machinery and equipment were negligible in that period.

Second, in this period many handicraft cooperatives and individual handicraftsmen were also engaged in the production of capital goods. However, it is extremely doubtful that any significant amount of modern machinery was turned out by those handicraft units. According to surveys, handicraft units manufactured such capital goods as furniture, simple tools, cutlery, farm implements, traditional oil-pressing equipment and milling equipment, wooden boats, fish nets, and so forth. Those items will be included in our investment components "office furniture and tools" and "other rural investment."

The last adjustment to be made for this component is to add the values of major repairs done by the machine-building industry in various years. Unlike the construction series, the output value of machinery and equipment in the base year, 803 million yuan in 1952 (776 million yuan plus 3.5 per cent for transportation), is exclusive of major repairs. Though this missing item must be filled in, to estimate it from official statistics is by no means easy.

The Chinese government differentiates three categories of repairs: major, medium, and small repairs. The dividing lines between the categories are only loosely defined in the official documents. While medium and small repairs are considered part of routine maintenance activities, to be included in current production costs, each state enterprise is required to set aside a "major repair reserve fund" to meet the costs of major repairs that would occur not every year but over a period of time. The government asserts that major repair works are similar to investment activities, in the sense that they increase the remaining value of fixed assets, although they do not create any physically new assets.[9] A "major repair" refers to the replacement or repair "on a large scale" of the worn-out parts or components of fixed assets; reroofing and replacing a heating system have been cited as examples.[10] Another official source defines major repairs as work whose cost exceeds 30 per cent of the original values of the assets in question.[11] This is not too meaningful either, because the original value of an asset may vary from 200 yuan to millions of yuan.

In the First Five-Year Plan, the amount of 3,600 million yuan was included for the expenses of major repairs over the whole five-year period. The Chinese planners apparently overestimated the needs for major repairs by a sizeable margin; it was reported that on the average about 400 million yuan a year was collected under the account of major repair reserve funds,[12] and an even smaller amount was actually spent. According to one official source, on the average about 42 per cent of the major repair reserve funds were unspent.[13]

From the Western studies that have estimated major repairs for Communist China, we have selected K. C. Yeh's figures to be used here, because he has taken into account the complications mentioned above.[14] However, Yeh's figures are for major repairs in the whole economy, and we must determine what portion of these repairs was done by the machine-building industry. Using the average ratio reflected in the composition of fixed investment in China during this period (for detailed analysis of this ratio see chapter 7); we arrive at the figure of 30 per cent for repair of machinery and equipment.

The addition of the figures for major repairs and the values of

9. *TCKTTH*, 1956, No. 15, pp. 19–20.
10. *MTCS*, p. 4, and *TCKTTH*, 1956, No. 1, p. 31.
11. Ishikawa, *National Income and Capital Formation in Mainland China*, p. 142.
12. *CHCC*, 1958, No. 4, p. 28.
13. *TC*, 1957, No. 1, pp. 11–12.
14. K. C. Yeh, "Capital Formation," in *Economic Trends in Communist China*, ed. Eckstein, Galenson, and Liu, p. 541.

output according to our index numbers gives the following estimated values (in million yuan) for domestic production of machinery and equipment:

	Output of new machinery and equipment	Major repairs	Total production value of machinery and equipment
1952	803	147	950
1953	1,072	162	1,234
1954	1,410	186	1,596
1955	1,862	219	2,081
1956	2,915	252	3,167
1957	2,471	294	2,765

3. NET IMPORTS OF MACHINERY AND EQUIPMENT

Figures in this category are net amounts; that is, exports of Chinese machinery and equipment are subtracted from total imports of machinery and equipment in each year. To be conceptually consistent, we try to exclude, whenever possible, parts, accessories, and consumer durables. Owing to the extreme paucity of trade data released by the Chinese government, we must depend virtually exclusively on statistics from China's trade partners.

Net imports of machinery and equipment are grouped into three subcategories according to origin: the non-Communist world, the USSR, and other Communist countries. Import data of the three groups differ in the degree of reliability and in the pricing basis.

The Soviet data are taken from the foreign trade statistical handbooks published by the Soviet Ministry of Foreign Trade. The commodity classifications are clear and consistent over time. The data are highly reliable except that they sometimes comprise transshipments and reexports of goods originating in Western Europe.[15] The Soviet data for this period are in old rubles valued f.o.b. the Sino-Soviet border.

Imports of machinery and equipment from the Soviet Union include "equipment and materials for complete enterprises," that is, package deals inclusive of installation costs. Fortunately, the inclusion of installation costs here does not create any problems of

15. Alexander Eckstein, *Communist China's Economic Growth and Foreign Trade*, p. 288.

double counting, because if the equipment was installed by the Soviet firms and technicians and the installation costs were charged to the foreign trade account, the costs would not be counted in the total value of construction and installation work done by the Chinese construction industry.

The quality of trade data for non-Communist countries is less satisfactory. We use the data compiled by the U.S. Department of Commerce and published in the annual reports of the Administrator of the Mutual Defense Assistance Control Act. Exports to China are valued f.o.b. sellers' ports and have been converted from the national currencies to dollars. Possible errors in the data may come from two sources. First, the data have not been adjusted for reexports, especially through Hong Kong. Second, "exports to China" reported by some non-Communist countries may have included exports to North Korea, North Vietnam, Outer Mongolia, or Taiwan.[16] Consequently, figures in this category are overstated by an unknown margin.

Imports from Eastern European countries have been derived through a more roundabout way. All Eastern European countries have published foreign trade statistics, but they are less comprehensive than those of the Soviet Union. More important, none of those countries has singled out the value of machinery and equipment as a separate category exported to Communist China for any year. However, four countries—Poland, Czechoslovakia, Hungary, and Bulgaria—have provided data on exports of major items of machinery to China in various years. So far, a total of thirty-five such items, in the form of more or less complete time series, have been collected. We use them to construct an index to represent the year-to-year variations in the total volume of exports of machinery and equipment from all Eastern European countries to Communist China.

Two problems arise in constructing such an index. First, we need prices or unit values of the products as weights so that the thirty-five time series can be combined. Second, all the values and value coefficients are originally expressed in local currencies; thus, we have to convert them into a single uniform currency.

16. Colombia includes her exports to Taiwan; Canada, Ceylon, Indonesia, Norway, Pakistan, New Zealand, and Australia include their exports to Outer Mongolia.

In the original sources the data on exports of individual machinery products are presented in four ways. (1) Some series are given in both quantities and values. (2) Some series are given in monetary values only. (3) For still other series, both quantities and values are given for some years but only quantities are available for other years. (4) The remaining series are expressed in quantities only for all years. So far as the weighting problem is concerned, the first two categories of data do not create any difficulty at all. For the third type of information, we can compute unit values from the years for which both quantities and values are given and apply the unit values to the other years for which only quantities are available. For most items in the last category, unit values are computed from the data provided by the Soviet foreign trade statistical handbooks. Let us take the trucks exported by Czechoslovakia as an example to illustrate our computational procedure and the underlying assumptions. There is no price information for trucks sold by Czechoslovakia to Communist China. However, the unit value can be obtained from the data on truck exports from Czechoslovakia to the Soviet Union, as given in the comprehensive Soviet foreign trade statistical handbooks. This unit value is then borrowed for our purpose. The assumptions involved are the following. First, trucks exported by Czechoslovakia to China and the Soviet Union are asssumed to be quite comparable in quality. Second, we assume that transportation costs do not create any complication. The unit value of Czech trucks recorded in the Soviet trade statistics is the c.i.f. price to the Soviet border. Since Czechoslovakia is contiguous to the Soviet Union, the Soviet c.i.f. import price equals the Czech f.o.b. export price. Since Czech goods have to go via Soviet territory, the same Czech f.o.b. price applies to the trucks sold by her to China.

After the weighting problem has been solved, all values expressed in different national currencies are converted into old rubles according to the official exchange rates. This is necessary not only because all values have to be in the same currency but also because Chinese trade with Eastern European countries has always been conducted with the trade ruble as the accounting unit. In fact, Communist China has never had "trade" exchange rates between the yuan and Eastern European national currencies except the Rumanian lei.

The index numbers so constructed (see Appendix table A-6) are incomplete in coverage, since they are based on selected items from four countries, and can be used only to represent the year-to-year variations in total exports of machinery and equipment from Eastern European countries. We had to find the total value of exports of machinery and equipment from those countries to China in some year so that we could convert the index numbers into full values. The statistical handbooks of Eastern European countries do give the combined total of all exports from those countries to China in 1953. The share of machinery and equipment in this total for 1953 is given by a Chinese official source as 51 per cent.[17] Therefore, we calculate that the value of China's imports of machinery and equipment from Eastern European countries in 1953 was 371.6 million old rubles.

Foreign trade statistics published by the Eastern European countries show that China exported very few capital goods to those countries. Therefore, we have taken the figure for China's total imports of machinery and equipment from those countries as the figure for her net imports.

For Asian Communist countries, namely North Korea, North Vietnam, and Outer Mongolia, we assume that there were no exports of machinery and equipment to China. However, there are indications that China did export considerable amounts of capital goods to these countries. China's exports of capital goods to the Asian Communist countries are believed to have been closely related to her economic assistance programs. The Asian Communist countries imported machinery from China because the goods were free or because China had specified that her loans must be spent to import goods from China. Therefore, crude estimates of China's exports of machinery and equipment to them in various years are derived from the figures of foreign loans extended by China to those countries, and from the amounts of their trade balances. The results are shown in table A-8 of the Appendix.

The figures for China's net imports of machinery and equipment from all Communist countries except the USSR then are obtained by subtracting her exports to the Asian Communist countries from

17. *HHPYK*, 1953, No. 9, p. 166. This is the only clue ever published by Peking concerning the value of machinery and equipment imported from Eastern European countries.

her imports from Eastern Europe. The figures are expressed in rubles.

The various import series derived thus far are values in rubles or dollars. Two special problems remain to be solved. First, they should be based on constant prices. Second, the values should be converted into yuan. With regard to the first problem, Yeh Chi-chuang, minister of foreign trade, has disclosed that prices of most commodities in Sino-Soviet trade were pegged for the whole period 1950–57.[18] It is also clear from the trade agreements signed by China and Eastern European countries that prices in their trade were generally tied up with the prices for comparable goods quoted in Sino-Soviet trade agreements.[19] Thus, we may be justified in assuming that China's trade with Communist countries was conducted, in effect, on the basis of constant prices during that period. Prices may have fluctuated in China's trade with non-Communist countries as world market prices changed. We have not, however, deflated this time series, because of statistical difficulties.

In solving the second problem, we have converted all imports of machinery and equipment originally expressed in foreign currencies into yuan, using independently computed conversion rates, because the official exchange rates (as we indicated earlier) fail to reflect the purchasing power parities between the yuan and foreign currencies and, moreover, are mutually inconsistent. For our purposes, meaningful conversion rates are those which approximately represent the actual purchasing power parities between the yuan and foreign currencies for the products of machinery and equipment entering China's foreign trade. Our derivation of conversion rates involves a rather complicated procedure and requires a lengthy explanation, which is given in Appendix B. Only the essential points involved are presented here.

The computations have to be conducted separately for the USSR, other Communist countries, and non-Communist countries. An official handbook for investment budgeting gives the original prices exclusive of transportation costs, expressed in yuan according to the official yuan-ruble exchange rate, for thirty-one types of

18. *HHPYK*, 1957, No. 16, pp. 90–95.
19. See trade protocols between Communist China and the Eastern European countries compiled in *Collection of Treaties of People's Republic of China* (Peking: Law Publishing House), various volumes.

machines imported from the USSR.[20] It also quotes the factory prices for the same thirty-one machines with exactly identical specifications but produced in China. Among the thirty-one pairs, the prices of Chinese machines are lower than the prices of Soviet machines in twenty-nine cases, higher in one case, and equal in one case. The unweighted average of the thirty-one price ratios is 141.5:100. Taking this average price ratio as an indicator, the official yuan-ruble exchange rate (0.95 yuan to the ruble) overvalues Soviet machines by 41.5 per cent.

Note that the Soviet prices listed in that handbook are exclusive of any transportation cost, whereas the Soviet statistics on exports to China are based on prices f.o.b. the Sino-Soviet border, that is, inclusive of transportation costs within Russian territory. The same budgeting handbook instructs the Chinese planners and accountants: "In computing costs, the transportation rate for machinery and equipment imported from foreign countries should be uniform, no matter whether from the Soviet Union or other socialist countries." [21] Judging from the rate table (see table 2), this uniform transportation rate outside Chinese territory has been set at about 10 per cent, that is, the differences between column (1) and column (2) in table 2. This means that we should raise our estimated average price ratio by 10 per cent—from 141.5:100 to 155.-7:100. In other words, the prices of Soviet machines f.o.b. the Sino-Soviet border, if converted into yuan according to the official trade ruble rate, are 55.7 per cent higher than the prices of Chinese machines with the same specifications. This in turn connotes that the

20. *JPRS*, 10913, Oct. 31, 1961, pp. 24–26.
21. *Ibid.*, p. 7. This sentence actually means that the transportation costs outside the Chinese territory are set at a constant flat rate for accounting purposes, because the total transportation rates for machinery and equipment from foreign countries are not the same in the table given in that handbook, due to the fact that the rates for domestic transportation are differentiated by region. Furthermore, the transportation costs for goods originating from Eastern European countries should be higher than the transportation costs for similar goods originating from the Soviet factories. The uniform 10 per cent rate is probably an approximate average, with the Soviet Union and all Eastern European countries taken as a whole group. In using this average rate, overstatements may be largely offset by understatements. Thus, we decide to use in our calculation the same 10 per cent average rate for both the Soviet Union and Eastern European countries. Otherwise we would have to furnish a rate less than 10 per cent for the Soviet exports and a rate more than 10 per cent for Eastern European exports.

official trade ruble rate effective before 1960 overvalued the ruble by 55.7 per cent so far as machinery and equipment are concerned. Based on this evidence, we set a new rate of 1.639 (= 1.557 ÷ 0.95) ruble to the yuan to be used as our conversion rate for net imports of machinery and equipment from the Soviet Union.

The new conversion rate is somewhat lower than most of the price ratios implied by the Chinese official studies on price comparisons for Soviet and Chinese machinery products. On one occasion a Chinese writer compared the prices of every type of forge hammer imported from the Soviet Union and the prices of Chinese products with the same specifications. The price ratio ranged from 154.5:100 to 245.0:100, with an unweighted average of 195.8:100.[22] Another Chinese study surveying thirty-three types of lathes concludes that "the prices of imported lathes are on the average 61 per cent higher than the prices of lathes domestically produced with exactly the same specifications." [23] A Soviet writer admits, "Chinese equipment is in most cases 1.5 to 2 times as cheap as imported machinery." [24] We take this to mean that the prices of imports are 50 to 100 per cent higher than the Chinese prices. Although these pieces of information seem to suggest a higher price ratio, we prefer our lower estimate because the other writers either have drawn their conclusions from less representative samples or have not specified the exact nature of the prices of imported machines, that is, whether they include transportation costs and service charges.

However, even our computed conversion rate, though more meaningful than the official trade ruble rate, is subject to some conceptual shortcomings. The specifications of imported machines and Chinese products compared in the above-mentioned studies or listed in the budgeting handbook are said to be identical. Even so, the quality of machines with comparable specifications but produced in two different countries may vary. Furthermore, the average price ratio we derived is an unweighted average of a small sample of machinery. There is no doubt that there were some ma-

22. *CHKY,* 1958, No. 6, p. 4.
23. *CHKY,* 1957, No. 8, p. 7.
24. Y. N. Kapelinskiy, et al., *Development of the Economy and Foreign Economic Contacts of the People's Republic of China* (Moscow, 1959), translated in *JPRS,* 3234, May 1960, p. 397.

chinery products that Chinese producers could supply in sufficient quantities, and there is an even wider range of products that China was unable to produce at all and had to obtain entirely from imports. A conversion rate computed in the above manner may overstate the purchasing power of the yuan, because the second group of products had an overwhelming weight in Chinese imports of machinery and equipment during her First Five-Year Plan period. It is also for this consideration that we have selected the lowest conversion rate among the different ratios suggested by various studies of price comparisons.

After the net imports of machinery and equipment from the USSR are converted from rubles into yuan, the 3.5 per cent domestic transportation rate must be added. In this period, 95 to 98 per cent of Soviet exports to China came by overland railway transportation,[25] and the Soviet figures are f.o.b. the Sino-Soviet border. There is no need, therefore, to adjust for transportation costs outside Chinese territory.

One more item, distribution costs, is to be added. The Ministry of Foreign Trade imposes service charges for handling imported commodities, to be collected by the ministry's trade companies before delivery. Yeh Chi-chuang and other Chinese sources have quoted the service charges as a flat rate of 2 or 3 per cent of the importation costs.[26] However, these are only approximate percentages; the effective rate of service charges varied in different years. Before 1957, service charges ranging from 1.5 to 3 per cent were collected on all transactions involving foreign exchange;[27] since 1957 a flat rate of 5 per cent has been charged on trade transactions only.[28] We have decided to use 3 per cent as the average rate for the whole period 1952–57.

The treatment of net imports of machinery and equipment from other Communist countries is similar to that of the Soviet imports. The same budgeting handbook quotes prices of machines imported from East Germany and Czechoslovakia,[29] which were then by far

25. M. I. Sladkovskii, *Oeherki ekonomicheskikh otnoshenii SSR s Kitaem* (A Sketch of Economic Relations between the USSR and China) (Moscow, 1957), p. 350.

26. *HHPYK*, 1957, No. 16, pp. 90–94, and *CHCC*, 1958, No. 4, p. 28.

27. *FKHP*, 1957, p. 59.

28. *Ibid.* Nontrade transactions are exempted from service charges.

29. *JPRS*, 10913, Oct. 31, 1961, pp. 24–26.

the two most important suppliers of capital goods to China among Eastern European countries other than the Soviet Union. For these products some comparable Chinese prices are also available on the list. Altogether fifty-one price ratios can be derived, giving an unweighted average price ratio of 157.9:100. A conversion rate based on purchasing power parity is then estimated at 1.662 ruble = 1 yuan (1.579 ÷ 0.95). This rate is then used for converting into yuan the net machinery and equipment imports from those countries.

The problem of transportation costs is slightly more complicated than in Sino-Soviet trade. In view of the relatively small size of Eastern European Communist countries, transportation costs within their borders may be ignored. There are indications, however, that most of the imports from these countries reached China via overland routes through Russian territory. For instance, the imports entering Manchuli, a border city in Manchuria, alone exceeded the total amount of Soviet exports to China each year.[30] This is perhaps the reason why the budgeting handbook set a uniform transportation rate for shipments from both the Soviet Union and other Communist countries. However, since the statistics of Eastern European countries on their exports to China are valued at prices f.o.b. their own borders, rather than f.o.b. the Sino-Soviet border, we must add to our values 10 per cent for transportation costs within Russian territory plus another 3.5 per cent for transportation costs within Chinese territory. On top of these we add another 3 per cent for distribution charges in order to arrive at the total costs to the Chinese users of the machinery and equipment.

The computations of yuan values for machinery and equipment imported from the non-Communist world differ from the two previous cases. That the official yuan-dollar exchange rate has overvalued the yuan is an undeniable fact. This has been most authoritatively described by Yeh Chi-chuang, the minister of foreign trade: "In our trade with capitalist countries . . . the prices of our import and export commodities, if converted into our domestic currency at the foreign exchange rate, generally have discrepancies from domestic prices, which have resulted in our losing in exports

30. Chen Chi-shih and Liu Po-wu, *Tui-wai-mao-i tung-chi hsueh* (Foreign Trade Statistics) (Peking, Financial and Economic Publishing Company, 1958), p. 144.

and gaining in imports." [31] The discrepancies are believed to be more pronounced in imports of machinery and equipment than in other types of imports. Unfortunately, there are no Chinese studies or even bits of information we can use to compare the Chinese domestic prices with world market prices of machinery and equipment. The only concrete clue close to our purpose is a price comparison for steel sheets. One Chinese source states that the price of steel sheets imported from capitalist countries, if converted at the official exchange rate and net of the 3 per cent service charge, was only 573 yuan per metric ton in 1957, as compared with the domestic price of 1,350 yuan per metric ton.[32] So far as this particular item is concerned, the price comparison implies that the prevailing official exchange rate between the yuan and the dollar overvalued the yuan by 136 per cent ($\frac{1350}{573} = 2.36$). Since steel is the most important material input in building machines, we have decided to use this price comparison to derive a purchasing power parity between the yuan and the dollar for machinery and equipment. Thus, instead of the official exchange rate of 2.345 yuan to the dollar, we use a conversion rate of 5.534 yuan to the dollar, which is the official rate raised by 136 per cent.

Note that our estimated rates of 5.534 yuan to the dollar and 1.557 rubles to 1 yuan give a cross rate of 8.62 rubles to the dollar,[33] which is surprisingly close to the standard by which the Soviet Union adjusted the value of the ruble in relation to the dollar in 1961. Under the Soviet currency reform effective January 1, 1961, 1 new ruble was exchanged for 10 old rubles. Externally, each new ruble is equivalent to $1.11. This currency reform in effect amounted to a devaluation of the ruble in the sense that, as a result, 10 old rubles = 1 new ruble = $1.11, or 9 old rubles to the dollar. This piece of evidence gives added support to our adjustments, which have not only put all the conversion rates on a basis of purchasing power parities but also made them generally consistent with each other.

31. *HHPYK*, 1957, No. 16, pp. 94–96.
32. *CHCC*, 1958, No. 4, p. 28. The import price plus 3 per cent service charge was 590 yuan.
33. If we use the rate of 5.534 yuan to the dollar and 1.662 rubles to one yuan, a cross rate of 9.19 rubles to the dollar is obtained.

As a rule, all exports from the non-Communist world to China have been valued f.o.b. the exporting ports. Practically all of these goods came to China by sea. Since there is no indication in Chinese Communist publications concerning the magnitude of seaborne transportation costs for imports from any non-Communist country, we have chosen to use a case study on transportation costs in German external trade.[34] This analysis has two merits especially appealing to us: First, it has estimates of transportation costs by commodity group. Second, geographically Germany may represent the center from which the exports of capital goods from the non-Communist world to China originated during the period 1952–57, and thus the transportation costs from Germany to the Far East may be taken as an approximate average for these countries as a whole.

The average seaborne freight factor for all German imports is estimated at 14.3 per cent of c.i.f. values; but that for imported machinery, which is of high value in relation to its weight, is only 0.9 per cent.[35] In view of the fact that the freight factor for all imports from Communist China is 15 per cent, slightly higher than the average of 14.3 per cent,[36] the freight factor for machinery between Germany and China is expected to be slightly higher than 0.9 per cent. It is also known that the insurance costs for shipments to Communist China, which is classified as a high-risk region, are higher than normal rates. Without specific information about the actual insurance rates for China-bound cargo, we arbitrarily set a 2 per cent margin for the combination of seaborne transportation and insurance costs for machinery and equipment imported by China from the non-Communist world. This 2 per cent is added to the import values originally stated on the f.o.b. basis.

Again, we add 3 per cent for distribution charges and a 3.5 per cent flat rate for transportation costs within Chinese territory to this value series in addition to the above adjustments.

The results of our calculations of the total value of net imports of machinery and equipment from the three groups of countries

34. Carmellah Moneta, "The Estimation of Transportation Costs in International Trade," *Journal of Political Economy* (February 1959), pp. 41–58.
35. *Ibid.*, pp. 46–47.
36. *Ibid.*, p. 56.

in the period 1952–57 are given in table 3. (The complex procedures and basic data utilized in each step of computation are presented in Appendix tables A-4 through A-11.)

Table 3

NET IMPORTS OF MACHINERY AND EQUIPMENT, *1952–57*

(in millions of yuan)

	From the USSR	From other Communist countries	From non-Communist countries	Total
1952	395.8	57.2	71.4	524.4
1953	389.9	217.7	124.9	732.5
1954	477.2	147.0	75.4	699.6
1955	535.8	138.7	71.4	745.9
1956	742.7	172.3	232.8	1,147.8
1957	652.7	122.3	413.8	1,188.8

SOURCES: Appendix tables A-4, A-5, and A-9.

No customs duties, it should be noted, have been added. The Peking government has promulgated regulations on customs duties, which set preferential rates on imports from countries having signed reciprocal trade treaties or agreements with China and regular rates on imports from other countries.[37] It is our speculation, however, that those rates apply only to a small group of private users, because no Chinese studies of investment costs or budgeting handbooks ever mentioned customs duties as an element in costs of imported machinery and equipment to state enterprises.

It should be noted that the time-lag problem arises again in dealing with imports of machinery and equipment. Some machinery and equipment imported in the current year may have arrived too late to be installed in that year, or some of them were held as inventories for a period of time. The failure to adjust for the time lag may affect the accuracy of our calculation of annual investments.

4. OFFICE FURNITURE AND TOOLS

As we noted in chapter 2, official investment data do not include the costs of most office furniture and small production tools, be-

37. Bureau of Customs, Ministry of Foreign Trade, *Regulations on the Customs Duties of the People's Republic of China* (Peking: Law Publishing Company, 1961), pp. 3–11.

cause these items fall below the value limit set by the government.[38] Nor are these costs included in the output value of the construction industry or the value of machinery output. Small tools are classified as products of the metal-processing industry rather than the machine-building industry, whereas furniture is produced by light industry or handicraftsmen. In order to achieve complete coverage we have to include both office furniture and small production tools in our calculation of fixed capital formation.

Table 4

INVESTMENT IN OFFICE FURNITURE AND TOOLS, *1952–57*

(in millions of yuan)

	Investment in machinery and equipment			Investment in office furniture and tools (4)
	Domestic production (1)	Net imports (2)	Total (3)	
1952	950	524	1,474	44
1953	1,234	733	1,967	59
1954	1,596	700	2,296	69
1955	2,081	746	2,827	85
1956	3,167	1,148	4,315	129
1957	2,765	1,189	3,954	119

SOURCES: Columns: (1) from p. 31; (2) from table 3; (3) sums of columns (1) and (2); (4) 3 per cent of column (3).

According to an official handbook for budgeting, "the purchasing expenses of production tools and furniture should be calculated at 3 per cent of the original prices of equipment and machinery."[39] Arbitrary and crude as this budgeting method is, it is the only clue we can obtain for estimating this item. We use 3 per cent of our estimates of investment in machinery and equipment in each year to represent the value of new office furniture and production tools purchased in that year. The results are shown in table 4.

38. In Communist China the cost of purchasing office furniture is treated as an item of operating expenses. CHCC, 1958, No. 2, p. 19. But in the West the conventional coverage of producers' durables includes office and store furniture and fixtures, office machinery and equipment, and cutlery and hand tools. See Simon Kuznets, *Commodity Flow and Capital Formation*, 1:21; and Henry Rosovsky, *Capital Formation in Japan, 1868–1940*, pp. 4 and 179.

39. *Standard Railway Design and Budget Handbook*, JPRS, 10913, Oct. 31, 1961, p. 8.

5. OTHER RURAL INVESTMENT

A large portion of annual investment in the rural sector was carried
out by individual Chinese farmers or by agricultural cooperatives,
and it has not been fully incorporated in the official basic construction data. In the draft of the First Five-Year Plan, a total of 10
billion yuan for investment, net of depreciation, in agricultural
production by farmers themselves was anticipated for the five-year
period (1953–57).[40] Of this amount 6 billion yuan was estimated
for fixed capital formation and 4 billion yuan for working capital
increments. At the end of the period, although several Chinese
writers still gave the 10 billion yuan figure,[41] at least one official
source quoted 12 billion yuan as an approximate amount of total
net investment actually made by farmers in that period.[42]

Neither figure can be employed by us, because the writers have
not broken down their totals into annual investments. Nor have
they furnished any information by which we can distribute the
totals into annual amounts.

More important, since we are using the commodity flow approach, some items of farmers' investment have already been taken
into account in our other component series. Theoretically, rural
investment should include the following major items: rural housing
construction, new water conservation and irrigation facilities, reclamation, farming implements and equipment, mature livestock,
and other investment in kind.

All large water conservation and irrigation projects are covered
in our construction series. This is reflected in the large amounts of
earth and stone work done and the large numbers of man-hours of
draft labor employed in various years. To the extent that minor
work to improve farmland and to repair existing irrigation facilities
performed by farmers every year may have been left out of our construction statistics, they will be rounded up in our estimated
amounts of other rural investment in kind.

40. *FFYP*, chap. 2, fn. 4.
41. For instance, *CHCC*, 1958, No. 2, p. 20.
42. *CCYC*, 1958, No. 1, p. 33. The same source also quoted (p. 27) 4
yuan as per capita annual investment by farmers in the five-year period. This
figure was probably derived by dividing 12 billion yuan by 5 years and then
by the estimated rural population.

We are confident that our construction series covers practically all rural housing construction. The official figure for total construction volume in 1952, which we used in computing our construction index for later years, is described as having a comprehensive coverage, including all rural construction.[43]

Modern farm implements and tractors are included in our series of domestic production or net imports of machinery and equipment. Domestically, these items are products of the machine-building industry, whereas most traditional implements come from other units, that is, from factories producing "metal products" and from handicraftsmen. Sometimes farmers make simple tools for their own uses.

The items of rural fixed investment that have not been counted in other component series will be grouped into three categories, each of which will be estimated separately:

RECLAMATION

Whether land should be classified as a capital good is subject to dispute in both Western and Communist countries. Objections to the inclusion of land in capital assets are particularly strong in the latter nations, not only because land is not reproducible and is not subject to annual depreciation in the conventional sense, but also because this inclusion would be contradictory to the Marxian labor theory of value.[44] Some Communist economists prefer treating land and underground mineral deposits similarly and assert that they command no extra value beyond the labor value spent in the process of bringing them to useful conditions. Therefore, they propose including the costs of reclaiming wasteland as part of fixed investment. However, in their actual investment accounting, the costs of reclamation are classified as an item of "expenses related to basic construction." For example, an amount of 300 million yuan for reclamation by the armed forces was so listed in the draft of the First Five-Year Plan.[45]

There is no doubt that farmland is productive; and an increase in it definitely leads to an increase in a country's production capacity. In order to achieve greater accuracy in our later analyses of

43. *TCYC*, 1957, No. 8, p. 16.
44. *TCKT*, 1957, No. 19, pp. 18–20.
45. *FFYP*, chap. 2.

the capital-output relationship in China, we have decided to treat reclamation as investment. In other words, reclamation is regarded as a special kind of "land improvement"—converting nonarable land into cultivated land. But this investment activity will be valued at cost, not at the sale value of the newly reclaimed land. Reclamation under the Chinese Communist regime has been carried out in two principal ways: (1) various types of state farms and state livestock farms, and (2) reclamation under the resettlement program. The total costs of reclamation include:

1. Housing construction in the reclamation areas
2. Purchases of equipment for state farms and state livestock farms
3. Construction of irrigation systems and reservoirs in the reclamation areas
4. Expenses of establishing tractor stations in the reclamation areas under the resettlement program
5. Labor costs and other expenses[46]

Items (1) through (4) are already covered in other component series. All we have to compute here is item (5), whose national average is officially given at sixty yuan per mou.[47] This figure, when multiplied by the total number of mou reclaimed in each year, gives us a series of "costs of reclamation."

INVESTMENT IN OLD-TYPE IMPLEMENTS, CARTS, AND
LIVESTOCK

These items are not included in the series of domestic production of machinery and equipment. Nor are they imported goods. The total value of those purchased by farmers and agricultural cooperatives in each year has yet to be estimated. *TGY* gives a time

46. See *CUCC*, 1958, No. 2, pp. 17 and 22.
47. *CHCC*, 1958, No. 2, pp. 22 and 23. I assume that this figure includes the expenses of moving people because as shown in p. 23 of that article, these expenses vary with the distance between the origin of settlers and their destination. It is recognized that whether moving expenses of settlers should be regarded as capital investment is still disputable. They are nevertheless included here because the proportion of moving expenses in this item is not known, hence they cannot be subtracted.

series for "total amount of means of production supplied to agriculture." [48] This category consists of a great variety of goods: (1) fertilizer, (2) agricultural medicines and their instruments, (3) modern farm implements, (4) water conservation and irrigation equipment, (5) old-style farm implements, (6) building materials, (7) livestock, carts, and producer goods for subsidiary works, and (8) other items. [49] Another official source gives the percentage distribution of these eight items in various years. Five items on this list are either current inputs or already covered in other component series we have computed. Item (8), although unspecified, is believed to represent some minor current inputs and is a negligible percentage in most of the years. Therefore, we single out the percentages of items (5) and (7) in various years and apply them to the "total amounts of means of production supplied to agriculture" in order to compute the quantities for our calculation.

A few words ought to be said about item (7)—livestock, carts, and producer goods for subsidiary works—whose percentage ranges from 22.8 to 36.7. First, because it includes producer goods for subsidiary works, it may duplicate certain things that have already been covered in other component series. For instance, some modern equipment produced by the machine-building industry for agricultural subsidiary works is included elsewhere. Second, the livestock are both mature and young animals; and the latter are not classified as fixed investment. In another respect, however, this item understates what we intend to measure. A large portion of the increments in mature livestock were not bought by farmers but were raised by themselves. Unfortunately, further refinements on these points are impossible. In my judgment, this item has a net bias in the downward direction.

IMPUTED RURAL INVESTMENT IN KIND

This is intended to be a catchall item for investments made in kind by farmers and agricultural cooperatives that have not been covered

48. *TGY*, p. 170.
49. Chu Ching, Chu Chung-chien, and Wang Chih-ming, *Wo-Kuo-Nung-Tsun Shih-Chang ti Kai-Tsu* (Reorganization of the Rural Market in Our Country) (Peking: Financial and Economic Publishing House, 1957), p. 41.

elsewhere.[50] It includes all self-made farm tools, house repairs done by farmers themselves, building materials locally collected by farmers and used for the improvement of their housing, and land improvement activities performed by farmers for their own or the cooperatives' land. Anyone who is familiar with conditions in Chinese agriculture is aware of the significant contribution of these activities to total rural capital formation. To ignore them means a serious understatement of total fixed capital investment in China.

Two sample surveys on income and expenditures of collectivized and individual peasants have revealed some information from which we can compute the average number of working days that a farmer spent on these unpaid activities in each year. From this average we can derive a figure for the total number of working days spent by all Chinese peasants, which is then multiplied by an imputed compensation rate per man-day.

Table 5

OTHER RURAL FIXED INVESTMENT, *1952–57*

(in millions of yuan)

	Reclamation	Old-type implements, carts, and livestock	Imputed investment	Total
1952	169	842	835	1,846
1953	140	1,146	848	2,134
1954	152	1,098	864	2,114
1955	267	1,139	1,053	2,459
1956	331	1,317	1,066	2,714
1957	541	1,161	1,080	2,782

SOURCES: From tables A-12, A-13, and A-14.

All the statistics used to derive figures for the three categories are presented in Appendix tables A-12, A-13, and A-14. Only final results are shown here, in table 5. The three estimates are added to produce the component series designated as "other rural in-

50. The Chinese Communist statistics for investment omit, as a rule, investments in kind by farmers. See *TCYC*, 1958, No. 5, p. 19.

vestment." This series is expressed in yuan, and no conversion is needed before aggregation.

6. SUMMARY

Our new estimates of investment in fixed capital in the period 1952–57, constructed with the commodity flow method, include five component series: (1) construction and installation, (2) domestic production of machinery and equipment, (3) net imports of machinery and equipment, (4) office furniture and tools, and (5) other rural investment. Each component has a nationwide coverage, and each one is independently computed. They are expressed in 1952 constant prices. Except for the series of imports of machinery and equipment, the basic data are primarily drawn from Chinese Communist sources. Statistics on imported machinery and equipment are those released by China's trade partners.

In making the five component series, we avoided double counting, and we did not include anything that is not classified as investment in fixed capital according to the conventional Western definition. In addition, a few valuation adjustments were made. First, in the construction series we made adjustments in order to compensate for the undervaluation of work done by draft labor.

Second, in determining the yuan values of imported machinery and equipment, we did not use the official exchange rates. Instead, we constructed new conversion rates on the basis of purchasing power parities of the currencies involved for China's trade in machinery and equipment. The new conversion rates are also consistent with each other.

Third, since conceptually we should value capital goods at the costs to their ultimate users, we must compute transportation costs and distribution margins, whenever applicable, and add them to the values of the component series. This was done on the basis of information provided by an official budgeting handbook. Although we used flat rates, we believe that pluses and minuses in individual cases are largely cancelled out in the process of aggregation.

Having derived the five component series and made all the necessary adjustments, we can combine them to form our estimates of gross fixed capital investment during this period. The results are presented in table 6.

Table 6

GROSS FIXED CAPITAL INVESTMENT, *1952–57*

(in millions of yuan)

	(1) Construction and installation	(2) Domestic production of machinery and equipment	(3) Net imports of machinery and equipment	(4) Office furniture and tools	(5) Other rural investment	(6) Total fixed capital investment
1952	4,789	950	524	44	1,846	8,153
1953	7,385	1,234	733	59	2,134	11,545
1954	9,401	1,596	700	69	2,114	13,880
1955	10,062	2,081	746	85	2,459	15,433
1956	15,622	3,167	1,148	129	2,714	22,780
1957	13,989	2,765	1,189	119	2,782	20,844

SOURCES: Columns: (1) see text; (2) see text; (3) table 3; (4) table 4; (5) table 5.

CHAPTER 4

Estimation of Fixed
Capital Formation
in 1958–65

THE PERIOD 1958–65 witnessed drastic economic fluctuations in
Communist China: production and investment activities at
breakneck speed in the Great Leap years, the ensuing precipitous
decline in nearly all economic fields, the sharp policy reversal during the readjustment period, and the resulting economic recovery.
While the general conditions in this period are well known, the
precise extent of the fluctuations remains to be measured.

Yet usable data are too scanty to enable one to make definite
assessments statistically. The flow of quantitative information continued in the Great Leap years, but the general quality of official
data for this period is believed to have severely deteriorated as compared with data in the First Five-Year Plan period. In order to
cover up economic failures, the Peking government decided, beginning in 1961, to forbid the publication of economic statistics
of all kinds—a ban which has been so effective that there is virtually a blackout on economic information about China. A few
percentage figures for individual items have been disclosed occasionally, but very often the quantities in the base years referred to
by those percentages are not made known. And even these few
figures represent only the brighter segments of a generally dark
picture.

Since the Chinese government's practice of suppressing economic statistics has been maintained since 1961, one suspects that it has become an established policy regardless of the prevailing economic conditions. If this is true, we may expect an information blackout for some years to come. Therefore, we must try to make some "educated guesses" about what happened in that huge country in this period, however hazardous the task may be.

Our methods for estimating fixed capital formation in China in the period 1958–65 must be different from the methods we used for the preceding period, in view of the extreme dearth of quantitative data. Needless to say, the methods for the later period are less refined, and consequently the results are subject to possibly larger margins of error. Because of the greater uncertainties in calculations for this period, we derive two sets of estimates, using different methods, and then compare them to determine which is more accurate.

1. ESTIMATE I

Generally speaking, we still follow the commodity flow approach, with the same five component series. Except for the series of imported machinery and equipment, use is made of the percentage figures which have been officially divulged in a piecemeal manner or have been gleaned by other Western scholars and this author in a painstaking process over the past years. These percentages have been linked together and converted, whenever possible, into absolute quantities or values. The missing links, unavoidable in this case, have been filled in by the author's own estimates based on some relevant information. Since to use those data involves a high degree of uncertainty, attempts are sometimes made to derive alternative estimates which may serve as checks on each other and form a rough idea about confidence intervals for our findings.

In the following sections we shall discuss separately the five component series of fixed capital formation and the details of their derivation.

CONSTRUCTION AND INSTALLATION

We were able to compile only two series of output of construction materials—timber and cement—for the years after 1957 (see table 7), and even these two series are incomplete. Furthermore, the figures do not show the severe declines suggested by other informa-

Table 7
OUTPUT OF TIMBER AND CEMENT, *1957–65*

	Timber (in millions of cubic meters)	Cement (in millions of tons)
1957	27.87	6.86
1958	35.00	9.30
1959	41.20	12.27
1960	49.00	n.a.
1961	30.00	n.a.
1962	25.40	7.12
1963	30.00	8.83
1964	n.a.	10.60
1965	n.a.	n.a.

NOTE: n.a. indicates "not available."
SOURCES: Timber: (1957–59) Chao, *The Rate and Pattern*, p. 130; (1960) *CKHW*, Oct. 19, 1961; (1961) *CKLY*, 1962, No. 1, p. 7; (1962) *CKHW*, March 17, 1964; (1963) *CKHW*, March 17, 1964.
Cement: (1957–59) Chao, *The Rate and Pattern*, p. 129; (1962) *NCNA*, Nov. 28, 1963; (1963) *JMJP*, Jan. 19, 1965; (1964) *CKHW*, Feb. 20, 1965.

tion concerning construction activities in the crisis years. The year of 1962 is known to be the lowest point, so far as investment activities are concerned, in the economic depression. Yet the quantities of timber and cement produced in China in that year are more or less comparable to the levels in 1957.

Although timber and cement are important material inputs of construction, their output series would not be good indicators of actual construction volumes in those years, even if we had reliable figures. During good years, when the economy is moving upward and construction is being carried out up to the physical limits of the economy, the availability of key construction materials undoubtedly sets a constraint. This availability may then be taken as indicative of the volume of construction actually taking place. However, when construction activities slow down, output of key construction materials may not necessarily decline by the same proportion, because part of current output may be piled up as new inventories, whether voluntarily or not. In other words, the availability of materials sets only an upper limit on the volume of construction and hence will be a good indicator of total construction activity only when the latter approaches the limit. In the Great

Leap years practically all reserves of building materials were completely exhausted under the fantastic investment drive, so that bamboos, clay, and other native or inferior materials were reported to have been used as substitutes for timber and cement on numerous construction projects. Therefore, there must have been an urgent need to restore inventories of the two items at least to their normal levels after the investment drive subsided.

We have also collected some quantitative information on construction of railways and water conservation projects in this period (presented in table 8). Railway construction came to a complete

Table 8

CONSTRUCTION OF RAILWAYS AND WATER CONSERVATION PROJECTS,
1957–65

| | Railways | | (3) |
	(1) Total route length in operation at year end (kilometers)	(2) New construction of trunk and branch lines in the year (kilometers)	Volume of earth and stone work completed on water conservation projects in the year (millions of cubic meters)
1957	29,862	1,166	2,974
1958	31,192	2,376	7,984
1959	32,500	3,136	n.a.
1960	35,000	6,000	n.a.
1961	35,000	0	n.a.
1962	35,000	0	n.a.
1963	35,153	153	191
1964	35,500	347	287
1965	36,000	500	660

SOURCES: Column (1), years: (1957 and 1958) *TGY*, p. 144; (1959) S. L. Shiriaev, *Transport Kitaiskoi Narodnoi Respubliki*, Moscow, 1962, p. 29; (1960) *Yearbook of the Great Soviet Encyclopedia*, 1965; (1965) *CKHW*, Oct. 6, 1965. Figures for other years are author's estimates.
Column (2), years: (1957 and 1958) *TGY*, p. 69, excluding special lines; (1959) *JMJP*, April 9, 1960; (1960) estimated by using the ratio of the increment in the total route length in 1959 and the amount of new construction in that year; (1961 and 1962) estimated; (1963) *NCNA*, Jan. 29, 1964, excluding forest railways; (1964 and 1965) interpolated on the basis of total route lengths.
Column (3), years: (1957 and 1958) Chao, *The Construction Industry*, p. 197; (1963) *CKHW*, Feb. 5, 1965; (1964 and 1965) *CKHW*, Dec. 18, 1965.

halt in 1961 and 1962; it was resumed in 1963–65, but on a scale that was almost negligible compared with that in 1957–60. This was probably also true with regard to water conservation projects, though the information is missing for several years. However, these two cases are again considered unrepresentative of China's general construction activities in those years. While overall investment was indeed scaled down sharply in 1961 and 1962, construction in certain priority branches of the economy, according to official reports, was carried on or even enlarged during the crisis years. For instance, the building of chemical fertilizer plants was assigned a high priority, and after 1960 the scale of new construction was increased year after year; in the textile industry, a crash program of investment began in 1965.[1]

What we have decided to use to measure the changes in construction investment in this period are a few index numbers of the volume of construction and installation within state plans, as officially revealed. For three years no such index is available, and we have made our own estimates based on other relevant information. The index series is extended to 1957, and the total value of construction and installation for 1957 (computed in chapter 3) is then employed to convert all the index numbers into values. The results are tabulated in table 9. These values represent the total costs to ultimate users, and no adjustment for transportation and distribution costs is necessary.

The weaknesses in estimating this component are that percentages of annual increases are available for just a few years and that the percentages are not useful unless they can be linked up with a year for which the absolute volume of construction and installation is known. The missing links have been bridged by our personal judgments based on some nonquantitative, circumstantial information. Therefore, the validity of the estimates can be established only after some consistency tests. As will be shown later, our estimates of the construction component, when combined with a set of reliable data for machinery and equipment, give reasonable shares for producer durables for all years in the period, and the investment structure based on our estimates is consistent with the known data on steel output. It should be pointed out that since our construction estimates are based on the linking up of percentages of annual increases, they stand or fall together. Conse-

1. *JMST*, 1965, p. 559, and *JMJP*, Dec. 18 and 25, 1965.

Table 9

VOLUME OF CONSTRUCTION AND INSTALLATION, *1957–65*

	Index (preceding year = 100)	Value (in millions of yuan)
1957		13,989
1958	166.0	23,231
1959	122.4	28,434
1960	98.5	28,000
1961	40.0	11,200
1962	50.0	5,600
1963	125.0	7,000
1964	140.0	9,800
1965	120.0	11,760

SOURCES: 1958: The input index for 1958 as computed in K. Chao, *The Construction Industry*, p. 57.

1959: *KCCS*, 1960, No. 4, p. 2.

1960: According to the original plan for 1960, which was supposed to be a continuation of the Great Leap Forward of 1958 and 1959, the total volume of construction and installation was to increase by more than 30 per cent in comparison with that achieved in 1959 (*KCCS*, 1960, No. 4, p. 2). Indications are that up to the middle of the year the plan was more or less fulfilled according to schedule, but the plan for the latter half of the year failed to materialize by a large margin because of the wholesale withdrawal of Soviet technicians from China and the rapid deterioration of economic conditions in general. For the year as a whole, the actual volume of construction and installation is estimated to be comparable to the 1959 level, that is, falling short of the original plan by about 30 per cent.

1961: It was announced in early 1961 that basic construction was to be scaled down, with major emphasis on finishing those projects that were nearing completion (*JMST*, 1961, pp. 238–240). By a careful counting of the number of unfinished projects by the end of 1960, the volume of construction and installation in 1961 is estimated to be only 40 per cent of that in 1960 (see K. Chao, *The Construction Industry*, pp. 60–63).

1962: In view of Chou En-lai's statement about a further cut in basic construction in 1962 and the announced number of projects to be carried out in that year, it is estimated that the volume of construction and installation declined by another 50 per cent in 1962.

1963: *CC*, 1963, No. 23, p. 5.

1964: It is assumed that the recovery gathered momentum in 1964 after the fairly good harvest in 1963.

1965: *JMJP*, Nov. 29, 1965.

NOTE: In converting the index numbers into values, we begin with 1957's value of construction and installation (13,989 million yuan) as given in table 6.

quently, they are quite sensitive to consistency tests; that is, an obvious inconsistency for any single year would provide sufficient grounds for rejecting the whole series. The absence of inconsistency in the tests we have conducted suggests that our estimates are reasonably good.

DOMESTIC PRODUCTION OF MACHINERY AND EQUIPMENT

An output index has been constructed for 1957–65 on the basis of ten items of civilian machinery. The index numbers are converted into yuan values by multiplying them by our previous estimate (chapter 3) of the value of new machinery and equipment domestically produced in 1957. Since that figure, 2,471 million yuan, included 3.5 per cent for transportation costs, it was the total cost to the ultimate users. However, we still have to add the estimates of the values of major repairs done by the machine-building industry in various years. The results so computed are presented in table 10.

Table 10

DOMESTIC PRODUCTION OF MACHINERY AND EQUIPMENT, *1957–65*

(values in millions of yuan)

	Output of new machinery and equipment		Major repairs (3)	Total production of machinery and equipment (4)
	Index (1)	Value (2)		
1957	100.0	2,471	294	2,765
1958	213.9	5,285	300	5,585
1959	364.8	9,014	300	9,314
1960	453.8	11,213	400	11,613
1961	207.7	5,132	440	5,572
1962	182.3	4,505	480	4,985
1963	274.7	6,788	530	7,318
1964	326.6	8,070	580	8,650
1965	396.9	9,807	640	10,447

SOURCES: Columns: (1) from Appendix table A-3; (2) since the value for the base year (1957) is known, the values of other years can be derived from the index; (3) figure for 1957 computed in chapter 3. In 1958 and 1959, under the pressure to increase output, many state enterprises postponed repair work. The overdue repairs were carried out only after the Great Leap Movement subsided. For the years after 1960, a 10 per cent annual increase in major repairs is assumed; (4) the sum of (2) and (3).

It is necessary to point out that the values of domestic production of machinery and equipment for the years 1961–65 are suspected to contain a serious upward bias, because the ten commodities used to construct the output index are "show pieces," so to speak, in the economic performance of Communist China in those years. The government has disclosed some information about these products simply because they were given a high priority during the period of economic readjustment and thus their production was relatively successful. Many other items of machinery, whose production was curtailed under the retrenchment policy, are not included in this index because statistics for them have been withheld. A glance at table 11 will support our suspicion. According to the index the level of production in 1961, a depression year, is comparable to that of 1958 but is twice as much as in 1957. Both 1958 and 1959 were years of the Great Leap. Yet output levels of machinery and equipment in all three years from 1963 to 1965 exceed that of 1958, and the 1965 level is even higher than that of 1959. In spite of our full awareness of the possible upward bias in the figures for machinery output for the 1960's, we are unable to discount them because it is difficult to find some appropriate standards by which to do so. However, we shall attempt in a later section of this chapter to reestimate this investment component by employing an entirely different method.

NET IMPORTS OF MACHINERY AND EQUIPMENT

In calculating figures for net imports of machinery and equipment in this period, we have followed exactly the same procedures described in chapter 3 for the period 1952–57. Briefly, there are four steps of computation. First, we divide China's trade partners into three country-groups. Second, for each country-group we compute net imports of machinery and equipment in dollars or trade rubles. Third, instead of Chinese official exchange rates, we use a set of new conversion rates derived on the basis of purchasing power comparisons between the Chinese yuan and the dollar or the trade ruble. Fourth, transportation costs and service charges of the Chinese foreign trade organizations are added in order to arrive at the costs to ultimate users of imported machinery and equipment. The results of these calculations are shown in table 11.

Two points have to be noted in connection with the fourth step of computation. After 1957 service charges on foreign trade transactions were set by the Ministry of Foreign Trade at a flat rate of

Table 11
NET IMPORTS OF MACHINERY AND EQUIPMENT, *1958–65*
(in millions of yuan)

	From non-Communist countries	From the USSR	From other Communist countries	Total
1958	338.1	795.0	543.8	1,676.9
1959	320.6	1,503.8	494.9	2,328.3
1960	289.7	1,276.1	533.7	2,099.5
1961	127.3	262.5	289.4	679.2
1962	71.5	26.7	77.9	176.1
1963	91.2	60.5	19.7	171.4
1964	348.3	114.1	20.1	482.5
1965	937.9	187.1	117.2	1,242.2

SOURCE: Appendix tables A-4, A-5, and A-9.

5 per cent.[2] We adopt the new rate in our computation throughout the period 1958–65. With regard to imports from non-Communist countries, we have used the same 2 per cent rate for the whole period 1958–65 to take care of transportation and insurance costs between the ports of departure and the receiving ports in China. It may be recalled that we derived this rate from the data on trade between China and West Germany, which is regarded as the central origin of machinery and equipment exported by non-Communist countries to China in the 1950's. This central origin, however, gradually shifted from Western Europe to Japan after 1960. Thus, to use the same 2 per cent rate overstates the average cost of transportation and insurance of imports from this country-group in the 1960's. However, the overstatement is believed to be negligible—no more than a small fraction of one percentage point—because in seaborne shipping a considerable portion of transportation costs are attributable to loading and unloading, which do not vary with shipping distances.

OFFICE FURNITURE AND TOOLS

Estimation of investment in office furniture and tools is the same as that described in chapter 3, namely 3 per cent of the total cost of machinery and equipment, domestically produced and imported.

2. *FKHP*, 1957, p. 59.

OTHER RURAL INVESTMENT

For the last component, other rural investment, there are relatively fewer quantitative data available for 1952–57 and practically none for 1958–65. We are forced, therefore, to resort to our own judgments based on known records in the 1950's and some circumstantial indications in the 1960's. In order to minimize error we shall consider the three categories included in this component one by one, because investments in those items are subject to different conditions and determinants.

Reclamation. Because of the high costs involved, reclamation of virgin land has always been conducted by the government. Especially important in this area has been the work carried out by demobilized soldiers to create new state farms. During 1958–59, the total area of cultivated land in state farms and ranches was expanded at a rapid speed, but after that it remained almost unchanged until 1965, indicating that reclamation activities under government programs ceased in the 1960's (probably owing to the financial difficulties confronted by the regime). Large-scale reclamation was resumed in 1965. Detailed figures and sources for our estimates of reclamation costs in 1958–65 are given in Appendix table A-12.

Old-type implements, carts, and livestock. For this period we have no information about the sales of these items. According to our figures, in the period 1952–57 this category showed a relative stability. Except for 1953 and 1956, the value was about 1,100 million yuan a year, which may be considered a "normal" level. Although it is implausible to assume that the same normal level of investment was maintained in 1958–65, it may serve as a reference point from which we can estimate the range of variation in the second period.

Theoretically speaking, this category of investment is affected by the following conditions: (1) As an investment item it must be a function of the general level of current farm income. (2) Ordinarily, investment is also a function of the availability of credits. In this case it is the availability of government loans to farm units for such purchases as implements and carts. This would be a more crucial factor when farm income dropped temporarily and the need to replace old capital goods was strong. (3) Since rural China has been communalized, the accumulation policy prevailing in most communes or production brigades is an important determinant. (4) Circumstances that affect the breeding of farm animals also affect this category.

The year 1958 saw bumper crops in most areas of China, and it was also the year when most of the newly formed communes implemented a very aggressive policy of setting excessively high rates of accumulation or sinking funds. The level of farm income began to decline in 1959 and 1960 because of crop failures. In addition, the government attributed the farmers' lack of incentive to the high rates of accumulation set in 1958, and it began to take corrective measures in 1959 by instructing commune managers to lower their accumulation rates. Undoubtedly, these factors had unfavorably affected the acquisition of farm implements in the countryside. However, part of the sinking funds built up by communes in 1958 must have been spent in 1959 and 1960 for farm tools. Investment in the means of production in the rural areas is believed to have dropped to a very low level in 1961 and 1962. On the one hand, farm income continued to decline as the agricultural crisis deepened; on the other hand, commune managers were deprived of their power to extract sinking funds after the reorganization of communes. Farm units probably borrowed small amounts of funds from the government credit organizations in 1961 and 1962 to replace the worn-out tools that were absolutely indispensable in farm production. So far as the population of draft animals is concerned, conditions prevailing in 1958–62, such as overworking, undernutrition, and lack of care, were not conducive to the breeding of farm animals.

Official reports mention that beginning in 1963 the government substantially boosted its supply of farm implements to the agricultural sector and extended an increasingly generous sum for farm loans to the rural population each year.

It is clear that most of the pieces of information mentioned above are not quantifiable. All we can derive from them are some orders of magnitude. In other words, by using the nonquantitative information and the "normal level" achieved in 1952–57, one may be able to tell the likely range of fluctuation in the second period. The level of investment in this category in 1958 undoubtedly exceeded the normal level by a great margin. But it probably declined rather rapidly from this peak in the following years until it reached, in 1961–62, a level that was barely enough to replace absolutely indispensable implements.

Imputed investment. There is no quantitative information about this category either. The abnormal conditions existing in the Great Leap Forward years and the subsequent crisis years also make it implausible to assume a constant per capita amount or certain trend lines.

In estimating this item we have used the pre-1958 levels as a reference point and made necessary adjustments on the following grounds. The amount of labor employed for capital construction on farms is largely a function of the mobilization pressure of agricultural units on peasants. This pressure reached its maximum point in 1958, when farmers were under the tight control of commune authorities; it was of a lesser degree in 1959. Labor mobilization was considerably relaxed after the reorganization of communes. Moreover, the activities may vary in accordance with the weather and crop conditions. In poor years more labor would have to be spent in combating natural disasters or rescuing crops. As a result, less labor could be spared for construction purposes other than repairing or replacing houses. Therefore, a minimum amount is assumed for 1960–62. As economic recovery began in 1963, the general situation in the countryside gradually returned to normal. In view of this fact, we have assumed the levels of imputed investment in 1963, 1964, and 1965 were equal to those in 1952, 1956, and 1957, respectively.

Our estimates for the three categories of "other rural investment" are tabulated in table 12. Although the estimation of the last two categories is admittedly weak, it is not difficult to determine the maximum effects of the possible margin of error on our estimates of total gross fixed capital investment (table 13). Our central contention is that, so far as the two items are concerned, the actual levels in the Great Leap Forward years must have been higher than those achieved in 1952–57 and the actual levels in the crisis years must have been below the 1952–57 average achievement. Other nonquantitative information would help us to narrow down the

Table 12

OTHER RURAL FIXED INVESTMENT, *1958–65*

(in millions of yuan)

	Reclamation	Old-type implements, carts, and livestock	Imputed investment	Total
1958	1,080	2,000	2,000	5,080
1959	600	1,700	1,500	3,800
1960	0	1,000	500	1,500
1961	0	500	500	1,000
1962	0	500	500	1,000
1963	0	980	800	1,780
1964	0	1,180	1,066	2,246
1965	1,200	1,540	1,080	3,820

SOURCES: Reclamation: From Appendix table A-12.
Old-type implements, carts, and livestock:
1958–1962: See the text.
1965: The sum of farm credits granted by the government in 1965 (*NCNA*, May 15, 1965) was about 33 per cent larger than that in 1957 (*CCYC*, 1958, No. 2, p. 4). It is assumed that investment in this item has increased by the same proportion between 1957 and 1965.
1964: Farm credits in 1965 were said to be 30 per cent more than those in 1964 (*NCNA*, May 15, 1965). This percentage of increase is used as an indicator.
1963: Total amount of means of production sold by commercial departments to the rural sector in 1964 was reported to be 20 per cent higher than that in 1963 (*EB*, 1964, No. 886, p. 7).
Imputed investment: See the text.

range in which the actual performance may lie. Even if our judgment is wrong, our knowledge about the achievements made in 1952–57 would help to set the limits of possible estimation errors. For the Great Leap years, it would be very unlikely for the sum of the two items to exceed our estimates by a sizeable margin, but a margin of one billion yuan may be allowed for toward the lower end. For the crisis years, the actual level is unlikely to have fallen considerably below our estimates, but a margin of 500 million yuan may be allowed for in the other direction. For 1963–65, a margin of 500 million yuan may be allowed for in either direction. As can be seen in table 13, therefore, the maximum effects of possible estimation errors on the overall investment figures would be somewhere between 1 and 4 per cent.

Table 13

GROSS FIXED CAPITAL INVESTMENT, *1958–65*, ESTIMATE I

(in millions of yuan)

	Construction and installation (1)	Domestic production of machinery and equipment (2)	Net imports of machinery and equipment (3)	Office furniture and tools (4)	Other rural investment (5)	Total fixed capital investment (6)
1958	23,231	5,585	1,677	218	5,080	35,791
1959	28,434	9,314	2,328	349	3,800	44,225
1960	28,000	11,613	2,100	411	1,500	43,624
1961	11,200	5,572	679	188	1,000	18,639
1962	5,600	4,985	176	155	1,000	11,916
1963	7,000	7,318	171	226	1,780	16,495
1964	9,800	8,650	483	274	2,246	21,453
1965	11,760	10,447	1,242	351	3,820	27,620

SOURCES: Columns: (1) from table 9; (2) from table 10; (3) from table 11; (4) the sum of columns (2) and (3) multiplied by 3 per cent for each year; (5) from table 12; (6) the sum of columns (1) through (5).

2. ESTIMATE II

As we pointed out earlier, our Estimate I of gross fixed investment is suspected to contain a certain degree of overstatement for the period 1960–65. The source of the biases seems to be the estimates of domestic output of machinery and equipment, because that series has been derived from an index which is based on a biased sample. To try to eliminate the biases, we shall use in this section a different method of estimation.

In this period, the Peking government has claimed, there was an increasing degree of self-sufficiency in machinery and equipment in capital construction year after year. The rising degree of self-sufficiency does reflect, to a certain extent, the improved ability of China's machine-building industry to manufacture a greater variety of machines with higher degrees of sophistication. But it also partly reflects the reduced scale of investment in the early 1960's. Nevertheless, the Chinese Communists were proud of their record in this area and thus did not withhold this type of information. From the official claims of self-sufficiency in machinery and equipment and the data on China's imports of capital goods reported by

China's trade partners we can make estimates of the supply of machinery and equipment from domestic sources.

However, in order to utilize the official data we must follow Chinese accounting practices. Only after the values of domestic production of machinery and equipment are reconstructed in this way may we apply our valuation adjustments.

First, statistically, the degree of self-sufficiency may be measured in two ways: (1) total domestic output of machinery and equipment versus net imports (i.e., gross imports minus exports) of machinery and equipment, and (2) total value of domestic production of machinery and equipment used domestically (i.e., total domestic output minus exports) versus gross imports of foreign capital goods. Judging from the way in which the Chinese Communists have used the term, it means the latter concept.

Second, in computing the degree of self-sufficiency in machinery and equipment, the Chinese must have used the official exchange rates as the valuation basis for imported capital goods. It is unlikely that the government made any adjustment for the valuation problem, such as we did previously.

With these understandings, we may carry out our computation, in the following steps:

1. We collect the statistics for gross imports (i.e., excluding imports of parts and accessories but not subtracting exports) of machinery and equipment from the three country-groups. The official exchange rates between the yuan and the dollar and between the yuan and the trade ruble are adopted to convert the three series of imports into yuan. For imports from the non-Communist world, 2 per cent for seaborne transportation and insurance costs between the exporting ports and China's importing ports, 5 per cent for service charges, and 3.5 per cent for domestic transportation costs within Chinese territory are then added. For imports from the USSR, only 5 per cent for service charges and 3.5 per cent for domestic transportation costs are added. For imports from other Communist countries, in addition to the 5 per cent for service charges and 3.5 per cent for domestic transportation costs, 10 per cent for transportation costs through Soviet territory is added. The results so obtained are combined in table 14.

2. Using figures for the gross imports of machinery and equipment derived above and the official claims of degrees of self-suf-

Table 14

TOTAL GROSS IMPORTS OF MACHINERY AND EQUIPMENT,
BASED ON OFFICIAL EXCHANGE RATES, *1958–65*

	Non-Communist countries		The USSR		Other Communist countries		Total gross imports of machinery and equipment (in millions of yuan) (7)
	in millions of dollars (1)	in millions of yuan (2)	in millions of old rubles (3)	in millions of yuan (4)	in millions of old rubles (5)	in millions of yuan (6)	
1958	62.5	181.1	1,218.4	661.0	1,030.1	614.8	1,456.9
1959	62.2	180.2	2,321.2	1,270.1	949.4	566.6	2,016.9
1960	53.0	153.5	1,930.5	1,047.4	999.2	596.3	1,797.2
1961	26.0	75.3	397.7	215.8	589.4	351.7	642.8
1962	16.9	48.9	75.1	40.8	222.6	132.8	225.5
1963	25.5	73.8	119.1	64.7	125.2	74.7	213.2
1964	67.1	194.3	195.5	106.1	125.6	75.0	375.4
1965	172.9	500.8	282.6	153.3	248.6	148.4	802.5

SOURCES AND EXPLANATORY NOTES: Column (1): from table A-4. The figures are exclusive of parts, accessories, and consumer machinery.
Column (2): Figures in column (1) are converted into yuan by using the exchange rate of 2.617 yuan to the dollar, and we then add 2 per cent for overseas transportation costs, 5 per cent for service charges, and 3.5 per cent for domestic transportation costs.
Column (3): From table A-5.
Column (4): Figures in column (3) are converted into yuan by using the exchange rate of 2 old rubles to the yuan, and we then add 5 per cent for service charges and 3.5 per cent for domestic transportation costs.
Column (5): From table A-7.
Column (6): Figures in column (5) are converted into yuan by using the exchange rate of 2 old rubles to the yuan, and we then add 10 per cent for transportation costs via Soviet territory, 5 per cent for service charges and 3.5 per cent for domestic transportation costs.
Column (7): Sums of columns (2), (4), and (6).

ficiency in machinery and equipment, we reconstruct the total amounts of investment in machinery and equipment as they would have appeared in the government's investment statistics.

3. Total gross imports of machinery and equipment are then subtracted from the reconstructed official values for investment in machinery and equipment to arrive at domestic production of machinery and equipment. As explained earlier, the results (in table 15) so obtained are the part of domestic production that was actually put to use in China. They do not include Chinese exports

Table 15

AN ALTERNATIVE ESTIMATE OF DOMESTIC PRODUCTION OF MACHINERY
AND EQUIPMENT, EXCLUDING EXPORTS, *1958–1965*
(in millions of yuan)

	Gross imports of machinery and equipment, based on official exchange rates (1)	Degree of self-sufficiency in machinery and equipment (in per cent) (2)	Output of new machinery and equipment, excluding exports (3)	Major repairs (4)	Total domestic production of machinery and equipment (5)
1958	1,456.9	78	5,165	300	5,465
1959	2,016.9	80	8,068	300	8,368
1960	1,797.2	80	7,194	400	7,594
1961	642.8	85	3,643	440	4,083
1962	222.5	90	2,002	480	2,482
1963	213.2	90	1,919	530	2,449
1964	375.4	90	3,379	580	3,959
1965	802.5	85	4,547	640	5,187

SOURCES: Column (1): From table 14.
Column (2), years: (1958) *HHPYK*, 1959, No. 19, p. 38; (1959) *CKHW*, Feb. 26, 1964; (1960) *CKHW*, Oct. 4, 1964; (1961) *PR*, Dec. 13, 1963, p. 22; (1962) *EB*, 1964, No. 892, p. 13; (1963) *ibid.*; (1964) *EB*, 1965, No. 901, p. 48; (1965) no official figure is available. The degree of self-sufficiency in 1965 is assumed to be lower than that in 1964 because of the enlarged scale of investment.
Column (3): For each year, let the degree of self-sufficiency be x, domestic output is derived as the value of total imports in column (1) multiplied by $x/(1-x)$.
Column (4): From table 13.
Column (5): The sum of (3) and (4).

of machinery and equipment. This series will be used as an alternative to our computation of the domestic production of machinery and equipment given in Estimate I.

4. Up to now, our purpose has been to derive an alternative estimate by reconstructing the official investment accounts. To complement this new series we need another new series of gross imports of machinery and equipment. The results in step (1) cannot be used for this purpose because the official exchange rates are rejected as meaningful valuation bases. Therefore, we begin with the same basic data on gross imports of machinery and equipment in foreign currencies and convert them into yuan according to our computed purhasing power parities. The results are given in table 16.

5. From the two new series of domestic output and gross im-

Table 16

TOTAL GROSS IMPORTS OF MACHINERY AND EQUIPMENT,
BASED ON COMPUTED CONVERSION RATES, *1958–65*

	Non-Communist countries		The USSR		Other Communist countries		Total gross imports of machinery and equipment (in millions of yuan) (7)
	in millions of dollars (1)	in millions of yuan (2)	in millions of old rubles (3)	in millions of yuan (4)	in millions of old rubles (5)	in millions of yuan (6)	
1958	62.5	382.8	1,218.4	806.6	1,030.1	614.1	1,803.5
1959	62.2	380.9	2,321.2	1,536.6	949.4	565.9	2,483.4
1960	53.0	324.6	1,930.5	1,278.0	999.2	595.7	2,198.3
1961	26.0	159.3	397.7	263.2	589.4	351.3	773.8
1962	16.9	103.5	75.1	49.7	222.6	132.7	285.9
1963	25.5	156.2	119.1	78.9	125.2	74.6	309.7
1964	67.1	410.9	195.5	129.4	125.6	74.9	615.2
1965	172.9	1,058.9	282.6	187.1	248.6	148.2	1,394.2

SOURCES: All data on gross imports in foreign currencies and the rates for service charges and transportation costs are the same as those used in table 14. But, instead of the Chinese official exchange rates, the following conversion rates are used: 5.534 yuan to the dollar (trade with non-Communist countries); 1.639 rubles to the yuan (trade with the USSR); 1.82 rubles to the yuan (trade with other Communist countries).

ports of machinery and equipment, we can derive a new series for office furniture and tools.

6. The three new series are added to the construction series and that of other rural investment as given in Estimate I. The results are called Estimate II and are presented in table 17.

3. TWO ESTIMATES COMPARED

Before our new estimates of fixed capital formation in 1958–65 are adopted for analysis, we must carefully examine their credibility. In addition to what we have said about the possible biases in the commodity sample underlying the computed values of domestic production of machinery and equipment in Estimate I, there are other pieces of evidence in support of Estimate II.

Of all the basic data we have employed for estimation for this

Table 17

GROSS FIXED CAPITAL INVESTMENT, *1958–65*, ESTIMATE II

(in millions of yuan)

	Construction and installation (1)	Domestic production of machinery and equipment (2)	Gross import of machinery and equipment (3)	Office furniture and tools (4)	Other rural investment (5)	Total fixed capital investment (6)
1958	23,231	5,465	1,804	219	5,080	35,799
1959	28,434	8,368	2,483	326	3,800	43,411
1960	28,000	7,594	2,198	294	1,500	39,586
1961	11,200	4,083	774	146	1,000	17,203
1962	5,600	2,482	286	83	1,000	9,451
1963	7,000	2,449	310	84	1,780	11,623
1964	9,800	3,959	615	137	2,246	16,757
1965	11,760	5,187	1,394	197	3,820	22,358

SOURCES: Columns: (1) from table 13; (2) from table 15; (3) from table 16; (4) 3 per cent of the sum of columns (2) and (3) in each year; (5) from table 13; (6) the sum of columns (1) through (5).

period, the series of imports of machinery and equipment is the only one that is on solid ground. This series is probably even more accurate in Estimate II than in Estimate I, because in Estimate II we have used gross rather than net imports of machinery and equipment, so that possible errors in estimating exports of capital goods to Asian Communist countries are avoided. Unlike in Estimate I, the series of domestic production of machinery and equipment in Estimate II has been derived from the import series; hence, it should be fairly reliable—at least better than the series derived from the output index. True, in describing the degrees of self-sufficiency in machinery and equipment the Chinese used only round figures; but errors due to rounding-off could not have exceeded 2 or 3 per cent.

The higher reliability of Estimate II can also be seen in table 18, which compares the total values of machinery and equipment, both domestically produced and imported, derived from the two alternative methods. The two estimates are virtually identical for 1958 and differ by only a negligible amount for 1959. This fact suggests that if the output index of machinery and equipment is constructed

Table 18

COMPARISON OF ALTERNATIVE ESTIMATES OF TOTAL INVESTMENT
IN MACHINERY AND EQUIPMENT, *1958–65*

(in millions of yuan)

	Estimate I	*Estimate II*	*Difference*
1958	7,262	7,269	−7
1959	11,642	10,851	791
1960	13,713	9,792	3,921
1961	6,251	4,857	1,394
1962	5,161	2,768	2,393
1963	7,489	2,759	4,730
1964	9,133	4,574	4,559
1965	11,689	6,581	5,108

SOURCES: From tables 13 and 17. The figures are the sums of domestic production of machinery and equipment and imports of machinery and equipment.

from a representative sample of commodities, the results obtained from the two different estimation methods should be almost identical. The growth rates of the ten machinery products included in our sample are probably fairly representative of the general situation in that industry in 1958–59, when the Great Leap Forward movement pushed up production of every item as rapidly as possible. However, the sample loses its representativeness for the crisis years; the total investment in machinery and equipment in Estimate I exceeds that in Estimate II by a sizeable margin for every year in 1960–65. Moreover, the implied degrees of self-sufficiency in Estimate I are much higher than the official claims, even after allowance is made for the difference in accounting procedures in the two alternative approaches.[3] There is no reason why the Chinese would discount the degrees of self-sufficiency if they were really so high.

Incidentally, figures in the third column of table 18 represent, theoretically, the overstatements in the estimates of civilian machinery output based on the commodity index: if they are subtracted from the figures in column (2) of table 13, a set of new

3. The degree of self-sufficiency of machinery and equipment implied by Estimate I is as high as 97.5 per cent in 1963.

estimates of civilian machinery output including exports can be obtained, as follows:

	Output (in millions of yuan)	Index
1958	5,292	100.0
1959	8,223	155.4
1960	7,292	137.8
1961	3,738	70.6
1962	2,112	39.9
1963	2,058	38.9
1964	3,511	66.3
1965	4,699	88.8

In comparison with what we have obtained from the commodity index, aside from the drastically scaled down magnitudes for the years 1960 through 1965, one can find a number of features in the new estimates. First, the peak level of output of civilian machinery was reached in 1959 rather than 1960. Output already had begun to decline in 1960. Second, both 1962 and 1963 were the trough, and the phase of upturn started only in 1964. Third, according to the previous series, annual output of civilian machinery during the crisis years was two to three times the level of 1957; the new estimates suggest that the output level at the trough was slightly lower than the 1957 level. Fourth, by 1965, output of civilian machinery had been restored almost to the 1958 level; this is quite in line with what is believed to have happened to other industrial branches in China.

There is something even more interesting about the new series. Since this series refers to civilian machinery output including exports, if we subtract from it the figures for civilian machinery output, excluding exports in table 15, column (3), we obtain an independent series of estimates for China's exports of machinery and equipment. It may be recalled that while we have collected detailed data on China's exports to the Soviet Union and non-Communist countries, there is no information about China's exports of machinery to Asian Communist countries. All we did was to assume that China's exports of machinery to Asian Communist countries might be a fixed proportion of her economic aid commitments to those countries. Now, we may use official exchange rates to convert the known values (in dollars or rubles) of China's exports of machinery to non-Communist countries and the Soviet Union back to yuan figures; and we then subtract them from our new independent series of China's total exports of machinery. The residuals would then represent China's exports of machinery to Asian Communist countries. The results of this computation are given below (in millions of yuan):

	Total exports of machinery	Exports to Asian Communist countries
1958	127	92
1959	155	82
1960	98	82
1961	95	81
1962	110	79
1963	56	15
1964	132	94
1965	152	100

As one can see from Appendix tables A-4 and A-5, China's exports of machinery to non-Communist countries and the Soviet Union witnessed extremely drastic ups and downs in the period 1958–65. However, our new estimates of machinery exports to Asian Communist countries, with 1963 as the only exception, manifest a remarkable stability, varying from 80 to 100 million yuan.[4] This proves that those exports were indeed tied to some contractual obligations of China. The year 1963 is exceptional either because larger statistical discrepancies are present in that year's data or because China defaulted on her obligations. As shown earlier, in 1963 the machine-building industry reached its lowest point.

All of the above considerations tend to support our confidence in the credibility of the trade statistics we have used and the machinery output figures we have derived therefrom. As long as statistics on one major component of investment are proven to be plausible,

4. If the official trade ruble rate is used, 80–100 million yuan can be converted to 85–106 million old rubles, which are fairly close to our guessed figures in Appendix table A-8 for this period except 1965. A comparison of these two sets seems to suggest that China was unable to meet her obligations in 1963 but made them up in 1965.

they may be utilized, with the help of our findings about the characteristics of fixed investment in 1952–57, to test the general acceptability of estimates of other components as well as overall investment.

Now let us turn to a comparison of Estimate I and Estimate II in terms of their implied ratios of producer durables in total gross fixed investment (table 19). According to Estimate I, the average share of producer durables in 1958–65 is much higher than the 26 per cent given in table 26 for 1952–57. Moreover, the shares computed from Estimate I vary in a wide range from the lowest (25.5 per cent in 1958) to the highest (52.7 per cent in 1963). These findings could be true only if the structure of fixed investment in the country had been drastically changed and all the underlying factors, including the general technological level of the new projects under construction, varied substantially from year to year.

Table 19

COMPARISON OF THE SHARE OF PRODUCER DURABLES
IN TOTAL GROSS FIXED INVESTMENT GIVEN
IN TWO ALTERNATIVE ESTIMATES, *1958–65*
(in per cent)

	Share of producer durables according to Estimate I	*Share of producer durables according to Estimate II*
1958	26.5	26.5
1959	31.0	29.7
1960	34.7	28.0
1961	37.2	32.0
1962	48.8	35.5
1963	52.7	32.9
1964	49.8	35.8
1965	49.2	37.2

SOURCE: Computed from tables 12, 13, and 17. Producer durables include "machinery and equipment," "office furniture and tools," and "old-type farm implements, carts, and livestock."

These puzzling phenomena are not present in Estimate II. The share of producer durables maintained a considerable stability from year to year. The average share in the early 1960's is higher than that of 1952–57 but by a lesser degree than in Estimate I. The moderate rise in the share of producer durables in fixed investment in the early 1960's may be explained by the following factors. As we noted earlier, construction of large water conservation projects and reclamation activities, which require very little, if any, installed equipment, were discontinued during the years of economic crisis. This may slightly lower the share of construction in total fixed investment. On the other hand, the period 1959–65 witnessed a rapid increase in the number of tractors used on farms. This type of investment involves no construction component at all. There are also reports that many Chinese industries were restructured to satisfy changed demands or the government's new policy in that period by remodeling or retooling, which again entailed very little construction work. For instance, between 1961 and 1964, more than one hundred large-scale factories making generators were converted to produce equipment for the chemical fertilizer industry.[5]

The rather substantial increases in the producer durable share in Estimate II in 1964 and 1965 are also in complete agreement with the known facts about China's economic construction during this period. What the Peking government did in 1961 and 1962 was not only to decelerate new investment (i.e., postpone the initiation of new projects) but also to cancel a large number of projects which already were under way and quite a few of which were close to the installation stage. Many such projects were resumed in 1964 and 1965, and the major part of tasks on those projects were installation work. That is why all of a sudden a large number of investment projects were brought to completion in 1965.[6]

The above comparison sheds some light on two aspects of our investment estimates. First, Estimate II is more credible than Estimate I because the former is consistent with the characteristics of investment in 1952–57. Second, our estimates of the construction component for the period are reasonably good; otherwise we could not have obtained consistent results even in Estimate II.

It may be desirable to test further the reliability of Estimate II. One possible way of doing so is to utilize the official data on basic construction. As was pointed out in chapter 2, the Chinese official statistics on basic construction within state plans are considered

5. *Shin Chugoku Nenkan* (New China Yearbook) (Tokyo, 1965), p. 211.
6. *EB*, Dec. 6, 1965.

to be of relatively good quality, because investment funds in this category come from government appropriations subject to the budget control and auditing of the government. Although the official data on basic construction are not directly usable as investment statistics because of their peculiar coverage and valuation basis, it is believed that there is a stable relation between the magnitudes of basic construction within state plans and the magnitudes of overall fixed investment in 1956–59, a time period in which the private sector of nonfarm production had been eliminated and the scope of state plans had been more or less established. Therefore, we shall compare the two sets of data for the four years (table 20). The closeness of the ratios of the two sets of magnitudes reinforces the confidence in Estimate II.

Table 20

COMPARISON OF BASIC CONSTRUCTION WITHIN
STATE PLANS AND ESTIMATES OF TOTAL
FIXED INVESTMENT, *1956–59*
(in millions of yuan)

	Basic construction within state plans (1)	*Total fixed investment, Estimate II* (2)	*Percentage of* (2)/(1)
1956	13,990	22,780	162.7
1957	12,640	20,844	164.9
1958	21,440	35,799	167.0
1959	26,700	43,411	162.6

SOURCES: Basic construction: (1956–58) from *TGY*, p. 56; (1959) from *JMJP*, April 1, 1960. Total fixed investment: from tables 6 and 17.

4. SUMMARY

Production and investment in Communist China fluctuated drastically during the period 1958–65. In addition, the information from China sharply declined in both quantity and quality. What few economic data are available may be unreliable or may have been chosen for release because they were favorable. Thus, some data have to be rejected as unusable, and many informational gaps have to be filled by our own imputation.

We have used the same commodity flow approach as in chapter

3 and have constructed five component series. Again, various necessary adustments have been made. The five component series are then combined to form aggregate fixed capital investment in the period 1958–65 (table 13). This set, labeled Estimate I, is the counterpart of the result in chapter 3 for the earlier period.

However, we have no full confidence in our Estimate I. Specifically, the series for domestic production of machinery and equipment is built on a commodity sample which is suspected to have an upward bias. The products for which the Chinese authorities have released production statistics could be "show pieces," those most favorable to their propaganda. Products not included in the sample could have been much poorer in production performance. Therefore, we construct an alternative series of domestic production of machinery and equipment, by using the amounts of imported machinery and equipment and the official announcements of degrees of self-sufficiency in producer durables in various years.

Once the series of domestic production of machinery and equipment is replaced by the new series, two other component series have to be adjusted. First, since the new series of domestic production, derived from the degrees of self-sufficiency, is net of exports of machinery and equipment, the series of imported machinery and equipment must be converted to represent gross imports. Second, the series of office furniture and tools must be adjusted slightly. However, the other two components—construction and installation and other rural investment—remain unchanged. After the same aggregation process a new series of total fixed capital investment is derived, called Estimate II (table 17).

Before we can conduct analyses of the period, we must compare the two alternative estimates and determine which one should be adopted. Five tests have been conducted, and they all indicate that Estimate II is much better than Estimate I.

As a by-product of testing the reliability of the two estimates, we have derived the amounts of China's exports of machinery and equipment to Asian Communist countries. These figures fully confirm our assumption that those exports were tied to some contractual obligations of Communist China, that is, foreign aid commitments.

CHAPTER 5

The Rate of Investment
and Its Fluctuation

FURNISHED with the new estimates of fixed investment, we may proceed to derive some inferences therefrom. It should be noted, however, that, given the nature of the data we have employed, our conclusions are tentative rather than definitive.

Under the First Five-Year Plan (1953–57), the Peking government tried to "marshall all efforts and resources for the development of heavy industry so as to lay down a foundation for an industrialized state and a modernized national defense." [1] The intensity of their investment drive is clearly reflected in the rapid increase in fixed capital formation, as shown in table 21. With 1952 as 100, the index of fixed investment rose to 255.7 in 1957. The average rate of increase was 20.8 per cent per annum. However, the acceleration rate varied enormously from year to year. The annual increase in fixed investment was as high as 41.6 per cent in 1953, the initial year of the First Five-Year Plan, but it slowed down in 1954 and 1955. Another sharp spurt in investment, 47.6 per cent, occurred in 1956, which has been described by Chinese economists as a year of "leap" before the "great leap" in 1958. This was followed, however, by a decline of 8.5 per cent in the absolute amount invested in 1957.

The tremendous acceleration in fixed capital investment took place mainly in the state sector. According to the draft of the First Five-Year Plan, the total amount for basic construction investment

1. *TKP*, Sept. 16, 1953.

Table 21

ANNUAL CHANGES IN FIXED INVESTMENT, *1952–57*

	Value (in millions of yuan)	Index (1952 = 100)	Annual change (per cent)
1952	8,153	100.0	
1953	11,545	141.6	+41.6
1954	13,880	170.2	+20.1
1955	15,433	189.3	+11.1
1956	22,780	279.4	+47.6
1957	20,844	255.7	−8.5

SOURCE: Computed from the data in table 6.

planned for the whole five-year period was 42,740 million yuan.[2] But the target was overfulfilled; total investment actually made in the five-year period was 49,270 million yuan.[3] Nearly 10,000 new projects had been constructed under the state plan in the period, including 921 so-called above-norm large projects.[4]

The effort made by the economy to mobilize savings and to invest may be conveniently assessed by computing the share of gross national product (GNP) that is set aside or devoted to capital formation each year. This share is often referred to as the rate of investment. To compute the rate of investment for Communist China is, however, complicated by the problem of selecting a proper set of figures for GNP. The Communist data on national income are not usable for our purpose because they refer only to net material product, that is, the net value produced by agriculture, industry, construction, freight transportation, the part of communications serving other "productive sectors," and trade and restaurants. For our calculations we have chosen, from various estimates by Western scholars, Liu and Yeh's gross domestic product (GDP) series as most complete and suitable.

However, slight revisions must be made in Liu-Yeh's national income series. Based on new information, their estimates of value-added in the construction sector may be somewhat understated. In addition, the growth rate of grain output in their study, which

2. FFYP, p. 22.
3. TGY, p. 55.
4. SSB, 1953–57.

has been estimated on the assumption that per capita consumption of grain remained more or less constant throughout 1952–57,[5] is considered slightly low in the light of a new study of grain production in Communist China.[6] Detailed adjustment procedures are presented in the Appendix (table A-16). The combined result of the two adjustments is not substantial, raising Liu-Yeh's 6 per cent growth rate for GDP in 1952–57 [7] to 6.6 per cent.

Table 22

FIXED INVESTMENT AS A PERCENTAGE OF GDP, *1952–57*

	Adjusted Liu-Yeh estimates of GDP (in millions of 1952 yuan) (1)	Value of gross fixed investment (in millions of 1952 yuan) (2)	Rate of gross fixed investment (per cent) (3)
1952	73,600	8,153	11.08
1953	78,220	11,545	14.76
1954	82,470	13,880	16.82
1955	86,590	15,433	17.82
1956	98,110	22,780	23.22
1957	101,530	20,844	20.53
Average 1952–57			17.80

SOURCES: Columns: (1) Appendix table A-16; (2) table 6; (3) column (2) as percentage of column (1).
NOTE: The average investment rate is the cumulated total of fixed investment in the whole period divided by the cumulated total of GDP.

Using the adjusted estimates of GDP, we computed our estimates of fixed investment as a percentage of GDP. The results are presented in table 22. According to these figures the rate of investment rose rapidly from 11.08 per cent in 1952 to 23.22 per cent in 1956, and only declined in 1957.

The average rate of fixed investment, based on our estimates, for the period as a whole was 17.80 per cent. Although this is below the rates achieved by many countries in 1950–60 (see table 23), it is certainly quite remarkable for a country with a per capita income as low as that of Communist China. For instance, China's rate is

5. Liu and Yeh, *The Economy of the Chinese Mainland*, p. 52.
6. Kang Chao, *Agricultural Production in Communist China* (Madison, 1970).
7. Liu and Yeh, p. 87.

Table 23

INTERNATIONAL COMPARISON OF GROSS FIXED INVESTMENT RATES,
1950–60

Country	Average investment rate (per cent)	Remarks
Argentina	22.9	
Australia	25.8	At current prices, including passenger automobiles
Brazil	14.5	At current prices
Canada	23.7	
Chile	10.1	
Denmark	16.9	
France	17.4	
West Germany	21.1	1950–59
India	13.0	
Israel	29.1	
Italy	20.3	
Japan	25.0	1953–60
Netherlands	23.3	
Philippines	7.2	
USSR	22.3	
United Kingdom	14.5	1951–60
United States	17.1	Government expenditures on equipment not included
Communist China	17.8	1952–57

SOURCES: Data for all countries except the USSR and China are from U.N., *The Growth of World Industry*, New York, 1963, various national tables; and U.N., *Economic Survey of Asia and the Far East, 1962*, Bangkok, 1963, p. 190. The figure for the USSR is computed from the data in R. Moorsteen and R. P. Powell, *The Soviet Capital Stock, 1928–1962*, tables T-44 and T-47.

significantly higher than that of India despite the fact that India received much more foreign aid. Even the Soviet rates were only 12.2 and 15.3 per cent respectively during their first and second five-year plans.[8] It seems that the Chinese Communist planners either attempted to outdo the Soviets in this respect or had a much

8. R. Moorsteen and R. P. Powell, *The Soviet Capital Stock, 1928–1962*, tables T-44 and T-47. The data are based on 1937 prices.

stronger urge to accelerate growth in view of the lower point from which China had to start.

What is really astonishing in the Chinese case is the acceleration of the fixed investment rate from about 10 per cent to more than 20 per cent in a short period of five years. In non-Communist countries, it would normally take many decades to accomplish such an increase in the fixed investment rate, which is more or less governed by the income level. Evidently, a totalitarian Communist regime with centralized economic planning is quite effective in removing this constraint on capital formation.

To some extent, the high investment rate in China may be said to be a result of her relative price structure. The relative costs of producer durables, especially machinery, are generally much higher in underdeveloped countries than in advanced countries. As Kuznets has demonstrated, the investment rate in Italy in 1950 was 19.2 per cent if Italian price weights are used for computation, but the rate would be lowered to 13.8 per cent if American price weights are used instead.[9] This possibility was further strengthened in China by the fact that the government deliberately set much higher prices for capital goods relative to consumer goods. For instance, in computing his investment estimates, Dr. Yeh applied two sets of prices to the same basic data. When 1952 prices are used, the average rate of domestic capital formation for 1952–57 is 24 per cent, but when 1933 prices, which were more or less free market prices, are used, the rate becomes 18.2 per cent.[10] If the differential between these two rates is accepted as a good measurement of the price effect mentioned above, our estimated investment rates in table 24 may have to be discounted by 20–25 per cent.

Another way to gauge the intensity of investment effort is to compute the ratio of incremental investment to incremental income in each year. Inasmuch as the bulk of the investment in Communist China is planned by the government, it would be appropriate to call this new ratio the marginal propensity to invest. (By the same token, the figures presented in table 22 can be called the average

9. S. Kuznets, "Quantitative Aspects of the Economic Growth of Nations," in *Economic Development and Cultural Change* 8, no. 4, pt. 2 (July 1960), p. 24.

10. K. C. Yeh, "Capital Formation," in *Economic Trends in Communist China*, ed. Eckstein, Galenson, and Liu, pp. 510–511.

propensities to invest.) For the period 1952–57 as a whole, the marginal propensity to invest was 45 per cent.[11] As seen earlier, fixed investment kept on rising and only declined in 1957. Thus, if 1957 is excluded, the marginal propensity to invest would be as high as 59 per cent. That is to say, more than half of the increase in national income was set aside for investment.

For the period from 1958 to 1965, an examination of our two alternative estimates has shown that Estimate II is more reliable. Thus it will be used here for analysis.

Table 24

ANNUAL CHANGES IN FIXED INVESTMENT, *1958–65*

	Value (in millions of yuan)	Index (1958 = 100)	Annual change (per cent)
1958	35,799	100.0	+71.7
1959	43,411	121.3	+21.3
1960	39,586	110.6	− 8.8
1961	17,203	48.1	−56.5
1962	9,451	26.4	−45.1
1963	11,623	32.5	+23.0
1964	16,757	46.8	+44.2
1965	22,358	62.5	+33.4

SOURCE: Computed from the data in table 17.

As table 24 shows, the ups and downs in fixed investment in a short period of eight years are indeed striking—a sharp contrast to the continuous acceleration in 1952–57. The year 1958 saw the largest jump, an increase of 71.7 per cent, in fixed capital investment in the whole history of the regime. The number of above-norm, modern projects under construction in 1958 was given as 1,135. This is even larger than the number for the whole First Five-Year Plan period. More astonishing is the number of small projects carried out in that year—about 40,000, or more than four times the number in the whole First Five-Year Plan.[12] Of course, most of the small projects built in 1958 were "indigenous" ones created to meet the pressure of the Walking with Two Legs movement.

11. For the five-year period, the increment of income was 27,930 million yuan, whereas the increment of fixed investment was 12,691 million yuan.
12. SSB, 1958.

As the Great Leap continued in 1959, another increase, of 21.3 per cent, in fixed investment took place. In absolute terms, the 1959 figure is the largest amount ever invested in China. In that year, a total of 1,341 above-norm projects were reportedly under construction. The number of small projects erected in the year rose to 75,000.[13] Fixed investment began to fall back in 1960, but only moderately at the outset. Construction on 343 major projects was discontinued in the latter part of 1960 because of the cancellation of technical assistance contracts by the Soviet Union and the withdrawal of Soviet experts from China in June of that year.[14] Presumably a number of other projects also had been halted later in the year either because they were ancillary to the Soviet-aid projects or because of the shortage of building materials. Drastic declines in investment took place in 1961 and 1962. Under the "readjustment policies" announced in early 1961, investment in that year was scaled down, with the emphasis on finishing those projects which were nearing completion. A low priority was given to planning for new investment projects.[15] There was a further curtailment in investment in the following year. According to the "Seventy Articles of Industrial Policy" secretly issued by the Peking government, unless special permission was given, all basic construction should be suspended.[16] There is no doubt that investment reached its lowest point in 1962. According to our estimates, fixed investment in 1962 was only slightly higher than that in 1952—a retreat all the way back to where it started ten years before. The recovery began in 1963, gathered momentum in 1964, and continued through 1965. However, the absolute amount of fixed investment in 1965 was slightly larger than the 1957 scale but only about half the 1959 peak level.

Our conclusions about the low investment level in 1962 and moderate increases in the following three years are quite compatible with the information about the general situation of production in China during this period. Theoretically, the increase in aggregate output of an economy is a function of, among other things,

13. *SSB*, 1959.
14. Editorial in *JMJP*, Dec. 4, 1963.
15. *JMST*, 1961, p. 238.
16. *JMJP*, April 17, 1962; and Choh-ming Li, *Industrial Development in Communist China*, p. 11.

the increase in productive capacity or net investment in fixed capital. When production is declining and excess capacity appears, there is no need for net investment, which would only create more excess capacity. Net investment becomes necessary when the economic recovery has brought production back to or near the full capacity level and further growth in output is desired. This relationship cannot be ignored even in a planned economy. As will be explained in later sections, when total output in China dropped to a very low level from its previous peak, there was probably very little net fixed investment in the aggregate sense. However, in individual sectors or industrial branches the policy of restructuring the economy had led to certain net additions to productive capacities in the priority fields and reductions in capital stocks in others. Some net investment, but still moderate in quantity, was made across the board in 1964–65, when the economic readjustment and recovery had been more or less completed and production was approaching its full capacity limits. Therefore, although total output in 1965 surpassed its 1957 level by a substantial amount, total fixed investment was only comparable to that of 1957. The timing of the Third Five-Year Plan is believed to have been based on the situation in the existing industrial capacity. It was scheduled to begin in 1966 [17] because the planners anticipated that by then industrial production in general would reach full capacity and any further expansion would depend largely on new investment.

A question may be raised with regard to the comparison of steel output and fixed investment in 1964–65. A Soviet source has estimated China's steel output in 1964 at 9.5 million tons,[18] which exceeded the 1957 level by 77 per cent. Yet total fixed investment in 1965 surpassed the 1957 magnitude by only 9 per cent. A number of explanations of this discrepancy can be found. First, as was mentioned earlier, there has been a shift in the composition of fixed investment toward the more steel-consuming components, namely, producer durables. According to our computation the value of domestically produced machinery rose from 2,765 million yuan in 1957 to 5,187 million yuan in 1965. Second, Communist China must have been desperately attempting to expand her capacity for

17. *JMJP*, Dec. 31, 1964.
18. *The Yearbook of the Great Soviet Encyclopedia*, 1965, pp. 282–285. It is assumed that 1964's steel output was used in 1965.

producing military goods, partly to compensate for the cutoff of military supplies from the Soviet Union and partly to meet her increased commitments of military aid to North Vietnam. Third, there was an increasing tendency in China to rely more on domestically produced steel. In 1957, 75 per cent of steel consumption came from domestic mills;[19] the percentage became 95 per cent in 1963,[20] or an increase of 27 per cent $(= \frac{95 - 75}{75})$. Fourth, some of the steel produced in 1964 may have been used for replenishing inventories. In the absence of concrete data, let us try to approximate the effects of the above factors in rough percentage terms just to see whether they can fully account for the divergence between the steel output growth and the investment increase:

1. Steel consumption in 1957 is taken as 100.
2. With other things unchanged, the 9 per cent increase in total fixed investment would entail 9 per cent more steel input.
3. The net effect of the shift in composition of investment may call for a 15 per cent increase in steel consumption.
4. The expansion of military goods production would require at least another 15 per cent increase in steel consumption.
5. The above factors add up to 39 per cent more steel consumption than in 1957. The 27 per cent increase in the degree of self-sufficiency in steel has cross effects on all the above factors. Therefore, the total increase in steel consumption would become 77 per cent (139% × 127%).
6. A few per cent may be accounted for by inventory increases, in case any one of the above factors is overstated.

The problem of inventory variations is indeed a crucial element in assessing China's economic performance in this abnormal period. Yet this issue has sometimes been overlooked by Western observers. During the Great Leap years, China had exhausted virtually all material reserves. The first two or three years of the ensuing period of economic retrenchment were too lean to allow the country to restore stockpiles of important goods to their previous levels; most of this task was probably fulfilled in 1964 and 1965.

19. *EB*, 1964, No. 889, p. 3.
20. *The Far East Economic Review*, 1966, No. 24, p. 6.

The inventory problem is important in both industry and agriculture. In food balances constructed for many countries, figures in the column "changes in stock" are usually either zero or negligible. That is, a more or less constant level of grain stock is maintained. This is true in a peasant economy in normal years, but it may not be true in a Communist country like China even in normal years. And it is certainly not true in any country, Communist or otherwise, in years of severe famines and years immediately after the famines. From the beginning the Peking government established a policy of grain stockpiling, with the aim of building up grain reserves sufficient to meet two consecutive years of serious famine. This policy is supposed to be implemented concurrently with the grain procurement program. The government's grain reserves were 1.18 million tons at the beginning of the 1950–51 crop year, rose to 12.69 million tons by the end of the 1952–53 crop year, and were 20.84 million tons by the end of the 1956–57 crop year. The reserves must have exceeded the 30 million mark by the end of the 1958–59 crop year. All the grain reserves are reported to have been used by mid-1961. Chinese planners obviously realized the great danger of operating a planned economy without any food reserves on hand. However, the crops in 1962 and 1963 were not large enough to remove their anxiety. The earliest opportunity for the country to replenish grain inventories was 1964–65.[21]

In 1964 and 1965 inventory investment was unusually large while fixed investment was only moderate.

For the period 1958–65 it is difficult to evaluate the investment efforts of the regime in relative terms, that is, to measure the share of capital formation in national income, because there are no reliable national income data, official or otherwise. The only conclusion that can be safely derived is that the rate of investment in fixed capital did not fluctuate as widely as the absolute figures of investment because national income modulated in the same directions as fixed investment, though by smaller degrees.

Even the appraisal of capital formation in this period according to absolute amounts is plagued by many complicating factors. Un-

21. Kang Chao, *Agricultural Production in Communist China*. All grain reserves are measured in terms of commercial grains whose conversion ratio with crude grains is 85:100.

fortunately, due to the absence of detailed statistics, those factors can be analyzed only in nonquantitative terms.

The first problem involves the quality of the capital goods added in this period and their effects on the increment of productive capacity of the economy. It is a well-known fact that numerous machines produced and many construction projects undertaken during the Great Leap movement were of very poor quality. Thus, investment measured in yuan may not faithfully reflect the real economic effects. In addition, there are other factors that necessitate the discounting of the measured investment in fixed capital. For instance, sizeable amounts of funds and construction activities in 1958–59 were devoted to Soviet-aid projects which were not finished by the time of the withdrawal of Soviet technicians and were thereafter abandoned. Unless construction of those unfinished projects was resumed in subsequent years by Chinese engineers or will be resumed in the near future, previous investment in them should be considered as wastage, because these projects never contributed anything to the productive capacity of the economy. The same may apply to those smaller projects which were discontinued because they were ancillary to the unfinished Soviet-aid projects. Judging from the number of projects so abandoned and their average size, the combined value of investment in them must have run into billions of yuan. Strictly speaking, this huge amount should be deducted from the investment statistics of the previous years or, alternatively, be offset by an equal amount of "disinvestment" or "extra depreciation" in the current investment statistics, because that part of investment simply had nil effects on the creation of productive capacity.

For the years 1960–63, one may find other types of "disinvestment" elements or "extra" capital depreciation, mostly aftermaths of the Great Leap. The important type was the scrapping of indigenous production units or tiny industrial plants that had mushroomed under the policy of "walking with two legs" in 1958–59. Unlike the discontinued Soviet-aid projects, those indigenous units or plants had been finished and did represent some addition to the existing production capacity. Yet they were either too costly in operation compared with their counterparts in the modern sector or capable of producing only goods of extremely low quality. Even some modern plants established in the Great Leap period were hastily designed and were constructed by local governments in their own territories regardless of the local situation of raw material supplies or other resources. They were soon proven uneconomical.

In short, those production units became obsolete as soon as they were completed. The scale of scrapping was surprisingly large, extending to all industrial branches. This happened even in the area of chemical fertilizer production, which is supposed to have the highest priority under the policy of "industry supporting agriculture." The following report from a Chinese official source may serve as an example.

In the city of Wu-shih, twenty-seven new chemical plants were constructed in 1958. During the first half of 1959, a rearrangement process started because these new plants were competing for raw materials. The quality of products was low and plants were too small. The selection of plant locations was not good and had bad effects on environment. Also, plants were so scattered within the city that it was difficult to supervise the operation. To rearrange these new plants, the first step taken was to consolidate those plants which were producing identical products so that the number of plants was reduced to seventeen. During the latter half of 1959 and the first half of 1960, the amount of output was increased, but inferior quality and lack of buyers forced those plants in 1961 to halt production one after another.[22]

Perhaps the most dramatic episode in this connection is what has happened in the iron and steel industry. According to official statistics, a total of two million small blast-furnaces were erected in 1958.[23] Most of them were the so-called backyard furnaces and very soon melted into piles of mud and bricks after a few rains. Others were discarded because of high operating costs and the low quality of products. By the middle of 1960, only three thousand such small units had survived after substantial remolding.[24]

The same type of disinvestment also took place in water conservation projects. Most of the small dams, reservoirs, and other irrigation projects constructed in 1958 had no adequate surveys in advance and no proper designs. Even on large-scale, well-planned proj-

22. *HHKY*, 1961, No. 23, pp. 1–16.
23. *CHCC*, 1958, No. 12, pp. 21–23.
24. *HHYP*, 1960, No. 20, p. 91.

ects, normal construction procedures were altered and precaution-
ary measures were abandoned under the pressure of speeding up the
work. A large proportion of water conservation projects built in that
year were unsafe or ineffective and very soon became inoperative.[25]
This can be seen from the officially published data on the total
area of irrigated land. The total area was one billion mou in 1958
and 1.07 billion mou in 1959, but it dropped to 550 million mou in
1963.[26]

In addition to the outright disinvestment described above, the
rate of ordinary depreciation of capital goods must have increased
sharply in the years immediately following the Great Leap, for several reasons. First, equipment and machinery in many industries
were overused or even abused in 1958–59. Some machines were op-
erated at speeds exceeding the technically permissible limits; commonly, regular maintenance and checkups were reduced to a minimum in order to gain more time for operation. Means of transportation were generally overloaded and kept running with little or
no normal maintenance. The impact of reduced maintenance and
repair on the average life-span of capital goods is felt only after a
certain time lag. It was first felt in the transportation system in the
latter part of 1959, when official reports disclosed that thousands
of motor vehicles could hardly be kept in normal operational condi-
tion.[27] Within approximately one year, similar problems arose,
with varying intensity, in other industries.[28] As a corrective measure, beginning in 1961, the Communist leadership launched a new
campaign urging all production and transportation units to place
a higher priority on maintenance of equipment than on production.[29] Furthermore, it should be noted that the shortening of
average life-span of capital goods also took place in the agricultural
sector. The most noticeable result in that sector was the soaring
death rate of draft animals due to overwork and under nutrition.

25. One official source relates, "There are in the whole country about 40
percent of the giant and intermediate projects, and about 30 per cent of the
drainage and irrigation machines cannot be commissioned for normal
use and operation." See *JPRS*, 30123, May 18, 1965, p. 45.

26. TGY, p. 130; *SLHP*, 1960, No. 1, p. 10; *JMJP*, No. 30, 1963, and
HKTKP, Oct. 1, 1963.

27. *CHYTC*, 1959, No. 9, p. 17.

28. *JMST*, 1962, p. 243.

29. *JMJP*, May 26, 1961.

Another factor affecting the average life-span of capital goods in the years after the Great Leap was the generally inferior quality of machines and equipment produced domestically in 1958–59. This was aggravated by the fact that in some of the factories that had been equipped with Soviet machines the cutoff of imports of spare parts from the Soviet Union made normal maintenance and repairs difficult.

In sum, all the aforementioned facts point to the necessity of discounting our measures of investment for some years in this time period, though the lack of statistical data prevents us from making such a quantitative adjustment. It is not unfounded to say that, in aggregate terms, the lowest level of fixed investment in 1962 led to very little net addition to total productive capacity in the economy. Even in 1963–65, the size of net investment must be regarded as moderate when compared with that in the First Five-Year Plan period.

CHAPTER 6

The Composition of
Fixed Investment

IT IS USEFUL to examine the technical structure of fixed investment, which not only reveals the country's development policy
but also sheds light on its stage of economic development. In table
25 we present the average share of construction and producer durables in domestic fixed capital formation for three groups of countries, differentiated by their per capita income levels. The computa-

Table 25

INTERNATIONAL COMPARISON OF STRUCTURE OF FIXED INVESTMENT
(percentage of total fixed investment)

Group of countries	Number of countries included	Share of construction	Share of producer durables
High-income countries	10	53	47
Medium-income countries	10	58	42
Low-income countries	12	62	38

SOURCES: Computed from the data compiled in S. Kuznets, "Quantitative Aspects
of the Economic Growth of Nations," in *Economic Development and Cultural Change* 8,
no. 4, pt. 2 (July 1960): 80–83.
NOTE: The basic data are those from the period 1951–57, at current prices. Kuznets'
original data are classified in seven groups of countries based on per capita income in
1952–54. Since the number of countries varies greatly among the seven groups, we
have regrouped them into three broader categories, each of which has approximately
the same number of countries:
High-income countries = Kuznets' $1,700 and $1,000. Medium-income countries =
Kuznets' $650 and $400. Low-income countries = Kuznets' $270, $200, and $100.
For each group, the averages are arithmetic means.

tion is based on data compiled by Kuznets for the period approximately covering 1951–57.

In spite of the differences in the share of construction among individual countries in each group (as influenced by factors such as the size of the country, climatic conditions, availability of coastal or inland water transportation, etc.), there exists a discernible pattern of fixed investment composition according to the stage of economic development. The share of construction tends to decline and the share of producer durables to rise as a country's income level moves upward. Three explanations suggest themselves. First, in the early stage of industrialization, there is a need for relatively heavy investment in overhead construction. Some overhead investments have to precede commercialization and industrial expansion and to accommodate the influx of people from the rural areas to urban centers. Second, the rising share of producer durables partly reflects the necessary structural change in economic development. In a less developed country, agriculture is the preponderant sector, and there is very little mechanization in that sector. The peasants use premodern, low-cost impliments. Therefore, the share of producer durables in agricultural investment usually is much smaller than that in industry. As a result of economic development, the importance of industry is bound to rise at the expense of agriculture; the average share of producer durables in total investment naturally rises. Furthermore, this share will be raised even in the agricultural sector, as farmers gradually mechanize their operation. Third, the rising share of producer durables also reflects the advances in technology in the industrial sector. As production technology progresses, producers tend to use more sophisticated equipment. The value of machinery and equipment installed per unit of floor space in factories tends to rise. Consequently, the investment share of equipment tends to go up relative to the construction share.

As Kuznets has pointed out, prices of producer equipment relative to prices of construction are much higher in the less developed than in the more industrialized countries.[1] This means that if the relative price structure in the advanced countries were used for all

1. Kuznets, "Quantitative Aspects of the Economic Growth of Nations," in *Economic Development and Cultural Change* 8, no. 4, pt. 2 (July 1960), p. 34.

countries there would be even more pronounced differentials in the shares of construction among the three categories of nations.

To investigate the Chinese case, we have divided our estimates of fixed investment into the components of construction and producer durables. The former consists of construction, installation, reclamation, and land improvement; the latter includes machinery and equipment, office furniture and tools, and old-type farm implements, carts, and livestock. The results are shown in table 26.

Table 26
STRUCTURE OF FIXED CAPITAL INVESTMENT, *1952–65*
(in per cent)

	Share of construction	Share of producer durables
1952	71.0	29.0
1953	72.5	27.5
1954	75.0	25.0
1955	73.7	26.3
1956	74.7	25.3
1957	74.9	25.1
Average 1952–57	74.0	26.0
1958	73.5	26.5
1959	70.3	29.7
1960	72.0	28.0
1961	68.0	32.0
1962	64.5	35.5
1963	67.1	32.9
1964	64.3	35.7
1965	62.8	37.2
Average 1958–65	68.9	31.1

SOURCES: Computed from tables 6, A-13, and 17.
NOTE: Producer durables include machinery and equipment, office furniture and tools, old-type farm implements, carts and livestock. All other items are in the construction component. The averages are computed from the cumulated totals.

The share of construction in China in the period 1952–57 varied between 71 and 75 per cent; the average was 74 per cent. This share is substantially higher than the average share in the twelve low-income countries in table 25. There is no reason to believe that the economy of Communist China in 1952–57 was substantially more backward than those twelve low-income countries. Therefore, this rather peculiar finding calls for more careful investigation.

Two possible explanations may be ruled out. Our investment computation does not contain a more complete coverage for the construction component than for the component of machinery and equipment; the large share of construction has been confirmed by many official reports. For instance, Ko Chih-ta puts the aggregate share of machinery and equipment between 20 and 30 per cent; another writer cites 30 per cent as the approximate share for machinery and equipment in the First Five-Year Plan period.[2] Nor was there any overpricing of construction work relative to machinery and equipment. It is well known that the Chinese Communist planners maintained a high price policy for machinery products during the period,[3] and that no such policy was set for construction work.

Several other possible explanations remain. To a small extent the unusually large share of construction may be attributed to China's special stress in this period on water conservation projects, which involve primarily construction work and very little installed equipment. Another contributing factor is the special accounting and statistical system used by the Chinese for compiling investment data. The Chinese planners classify all installation of machinery and equipment as part of construction, that is, under the general heading "construction and installation." However, in non-Communist countries machinery and equipment are often installed by the suppliers or some specialized firms, and the installation costs are included in the total costs of machinery and equipment. Unfortunately, the average share of installation costs is not known for either China or non-Communist countries. If the share is assumed to be about 10 per cent of the purchase value of machinery and equipment, the share of construction in China should then be reduced by 2.5 to 3 per cent.

2. Ko Chih-ta, *Kuo-tu shih-chi ti chung-kuo yu-suan* (The Chinese Budget in Transitional Period) (Peking: Public Finance Publishing House, 1957), pp. 109–110. *TC*, No. 3, 1957, p. 12.

3. The Five-Anti campaign against private industry and trade in 1952 seriously depressed prices of consumer goods but had little effect on prices of producer goods. The 1952 prices were later taken by the planners as constant prices, creating a pattern in which producer goods were overpriced in relation to consumer goods.

Perhaps a more important explanation of the high construction share is that the magnitude of fixed investment was suddenly accelerated during this period. For a given project, the shares of construction and equipment are determined by technical requirements. As a rule, construction work begins first and the installation of equipment will be done sometime later. For a country as a whole, these shares are jointly determined by technical requirements and the structure of demand. However, when the country is taken as a whole, because of the time sequence of the two components, these shares shown in investment statistics would be distorted by a sudden and big acceleration in investment.

Let us explain this point by taking a simplified hypothetical case. Suppose in the country the shares of construction and equipment in fixed investment, as technically required, are 65:35. And let us assume that on the average machinery and equipment are installed one year after construction began. A numerical illustration is presented as follows:

Year	Value of construction	Value of equipment	Total fixed investment	Share of construction	Share of equipment
One	65				
Two	65	35	100	65	35
Three	65	35	100	65	35
Four	95	35	130	73	27
Five	118	51	169	70	30
Six	156	64	220	70	30

If the annual investment level is maintained constant, such as in years two and three, the statistical shares of the two components reflect exactly the shares as technically required. In year four, 35 units of equipment have to be installed for the 65 units of construction carried out in the preceding year. When, however, the country suddenly accelerates its fixed investment by 30 per cent in year four, the construction to be carried out in this year then becomes 95 units. Because of the sudden acceleration of investment the statistical shares of the two components in year four become 73:27. In year five and year six, fixed investment is increased again by 30 per cent each time, namely, a constant rate of increase, and the statistical share of the construction component is then stabilized at the level of 70 per cent, which is lower than the share in year four but higher than what is technically required.

Furthermore, with investment rising year after year, the longer the time lag between construction and equipment installation the greater the distortion in the component shares. If the time lag in the above numerical example is extended from one year to two years, the value of construction in year five rises to 118 while the value of equipment remains at 35. The relative shares for the two components will then become 78:22.

These distorting effects are especially observable if one concentrates on the data on fixed investment in the state sector. This is so for a number of reasons. First, there are relatively more rigid technical requirements for this category of investment. Second, practically all large construction projects involving long gestation periods belonged in this category. Third, acceleration took place mainly in state investment. The relative shares of the two components in state investment were stipulated as 62:38 in the original First Five-Year Plan.[4] Apparently this ratio referred to the so-called technical requirement for investment composition. But when the state investment was carried out in an accelerating manner, the relative shares were completely distorted. Let us examine the breakdown of data on "gross additions to the value of fixed assets" in the state sector (in millions of yuan, at current prices):[5]

	Gross addition to fixed assets	Value of construction and installation	(2) as percentage of (1)
	(1)	(2)	(3)
1952	3,110	2,007	64.5
1953	6,560	5,350	81.6
1954	7,370	5,620	76.3
1955	8,020	5,550	69.2
1956	11,160	8,550	76.6

As we know, the acceleration of state investment in fixed capital began in 1953, the initial year of the First Five-Year Plan. The amount jumped by 111 per cent—from 3,110 million yuan to 6,560 million yuan. As a result, the share of construction for that year

4. JMST, 1956, p. 229.
5. From Nai-ruenn Chen, Chinese Economic Statistics: A Handbook for Mainland China, p. 162.

reached an all-time high. It fell back thereafter, as the acceleration rate of state investment in fixed capital declined. But the share rose again in 1956, when investment was increased by 39 per cent—from 8,020 to 11,160 million yuan. Moreover, water conservation construction reached an unprecedented scale in 1956; the total volume of earth work done in 1956 on water conservation projects was more than double that in 1955.

The above explanation for the years 1952–57 is fully applicable to the situation in 1958–65, except in a reversed direction. There are also additional complicating factors for that period. The construction share varied from 64.5 to 73.5 per cent, with an average of 68.9 per cent, which is significantly lower than the average in the preceding period.

The most conspicuous features of capital formation in 1958 and 1959 were the Great Leap Forward and the Walking with Two Legs movements, which had various impacts on the structure of fixed investment. The Great Leap Forward meant a sudden, tremendous acceleration in investment and production. According to the official figures, basic construction investment within and outside the state plan rose from 13.8 billion yuan in 1957 to 26.7 billion yuan in 1958, a jump of nearly 100 per cent.[6] The amount reached 33.4 billion yuan in 1959, which represents, however, a much lower rate of acceleration.[7]

In spite of the big boost in investment, the share of producer durables in 1958 and 1959 remained above the level reached in 1954–57. This is so because the Walking with Two Legs policy greatly reduced the average gestation period of investment projects undertaken in 1958 and 1959. As was noted earlier, about 40,000 small projects were constructed in 1958, and the number became 75,000 in 1959.[8] For most of those small projects construction could be completed and equipment installed within a few months. Therefore, the relative shares of the construction component and producer durables in 1958 and 1959 were influenced more by the low technical level of investment projects than by the acceleration effect described earlier.

The story for 1960–62 is quite different. This was a period of

6. *TGY*, p. 55.
7. *CHYTC*, 1960, No. 1, p. 29.
8. *SSB*, 1958, and 1959.

economic readjustment, with fixed investment sharply declining each year. In the latter part of 1960 construction on many Soviet-aid projects was discontinued. As the economic crisis deepened, the Peking government announced further cuts in investment; only the projects near completion received funds. Consequently, the share of construction went down. Accompanying the general curtailment of funds was a shifted emphasis in investment. It has been reported that many Chinese industries were restructured in those years to satisfy changed demands or the government's new policy by remodeling or retooling. For instance, between 1961 and 1964 more than one hundred large-scale factories making generators were converted to produce equipment for the chemical fertilizer industry.[9] Remodeling and retooling ordinarily entail very little construction work.

Acceleration in fixed investment was resumed in 1963–65. But its impact on the structure of investment was opposite to what occurred in 1952–57. A large proportion of investment activity in 1963–65 was devoted to completing those projects which had been discontinued in the crisis years. Consequently, the share of producer durables appears to have been abnormally high in 1964 and 1965.

9. *Shin Chugoku Nenkan* (Tokyo, 1965), p. 211.

CHAPTER 7

Allocation of Gross Fixed
Investment in Various
Economic Sectors

IN THIS CHAPTER we shall examine gross fixed investments made by the various economic sectors. Special attention will be given to the comparison of industrial investment and agricultural investment. There is a widespread impression that, during the First Five-Year Plan period as well as the Great Leap years, the Peking government's desire to industrialize the country as rapidly as possible meant denying the agricultural sector investment funds. Although this observation is generally correct so far as the state investment plan in that period is concerned, it does not represent the whole picture. An official source reports that a total of 7.4 billion yuan, or 8.6 per cent of the total basic construction investment within and outside state plans was allocated to agriculture, forestry, water conservation, and meteorology in 1952–58, in contrast with 44 billion yuan, or 51.1 per cent, for industry.[1] The 7.4 billion yuan, when converted into an average annual investment, is less than 1.5 per cent of gross domestic product in that period. This small percentage cannot be accepted, even intuitively, as a good indicator of the total gross fixed investment going into agriculture. During the First Five-Year Plan period 37 to 46 per cent of total gross domestic product originated from agriculture.[2] The tiny gross fixed invest-

1. *TGY*, pp. 57 and 59.
2. Liu and Yeh, *The Economy of the Chinese Mainland*, p. 66.

ment mentioned above is far from enough to meet even the capital replacement needs in such a huge sector of the economy.

That the bulk of agricultural investment has been excluded from the Chinese government statistics becomes quite obvious in a comparison of agricultural investment in basic construction within and outside state plans. As can be seen from table 27, for water conservation there was no basic construction investment outside the state plan in 1954, and the amount varied from 8 million yuan to 104 million yuan in other years—the differences between column (4) and column (6). Evidently, the official statistics include only major water conservation projects carried out within and outside state plans in each year and exclude the minor works done by peasants every year for the same purpose. With regard to basic construction investment in agriculture, forestry, and meteorology, the amounts within state plans and those within and outside state plans are identical for 1952, 1955, and 1956, and almost so for 1953—comparing the sums of columns (1), (2), and (3) with column (5). There is almost no investment reported outside state plans. The magnitudes of basic construction investment in the three fields are barely enough to account for office buildings, other structures, and equipment in the newly established government organizations and state enterprises in these fields, plus purchases of tractors and other farm machines.

In fact, the government on several occasions has explicitly mentioned the possibly large amounts of investment made by peasants and agricultural production units out of their own funds. There are also two specific estimates made by the planners about the magnitude of net investment by farmers during the whole period 1953–57; one is 10 billion yuan and the other is 12 billion yuan. The latter figure is perhaps a revision of the former. Out of this total net investment, 60 per cent is estimated to be for fixed capital and 40 per cent for working capital increases.[3] If we divide the 12 billion yuan according to these percentages, the net fixed investment is then 7.2 billion yuan for the whole period. According to yet another official source, the net rural investment in fixed capital in this period was only 40 per cent of gross fixed investment in that sector.[4] In other words, 60 per cent of the gross investment in

3. *FFYP*, chap. 2, fn. 4.
4. *TCYC*, 1958, No. 6, pp. 29–32.

fixed capital was for the purpose of replacing worn-out assets. This proportion of capital replacement in total rural investment is not unreasonably high; it in fact reflects quite truthfully the low rate of capital formation in the rural sector during that period. With a few yuan of investment by each peasant each year, one can hardly expect much to be left after the necessary expenses of replacing old houses and farm implements are deducted. If we accept 40 per cent as the net fixed investment in total fixed investment, the latter can be estimated at 18 billion yuan (7.2 billion yuan ÷ 0.4) in the whole period.

For the reasons mentioned above we need to compute the distribution of overall gross fixed investment among various economic sectors. Unfortunately, this cannot be done in the framework of our five investment components, because they are not broken down by sector. A rather roundabout procedure has to be employed, and for 1952–57 only.

First, we must try to single out fixed investment in the farm sector from our estimates of overall fixed investment. After the credibility of the estimates for this particular category is examined and established we can then proceed to distribute nonfarm investment among other sectors.

We begin with basic construction investment within state plans in agriculture, forestry, meteorology, and water conservation, as presented in table 27, because its definition and coverage are clear to us. We assume that, except for water conservation, official investment statistics in this category involve minimal distortions stemming from exchange rates and the inclusion of ancillary expenses, because of the nature of the capital goods needed for this sector. Thus, no adjustment is necessary. However, the official amounts of water conservation investment within state plans are raised to include the underpayments of draft labor in various years. In addition, we add the following items which are clearly excluded from the state plans:

1. Rural housing construction
2. Modern farm implements sold to peasants and cooperatives
3. Old-type implements, carts, and livestock purchased by peasants and cooperatives
4. Other imputed investment made by farmers, mainly their labor contributions to capital construction outside state plans

Table 27

BASIC CONSTRUCTION INVESTMENT IN AGRICULTURE, FORESTRY,
METEOROLOGY, AND WATER CONSERVATION, *1952–58*

(in millions of yuan)

	Within state plan				Within and outside state plan	
	Agri-culture (1)	*Forestry* (2)	*Meteor-ology* (3)	*Water conservation* (4)	*Agriculture, forestry, and meteor-ology* (5)	*Water conserva-tion* (6)
1952	186	3	0	331	190	410
1953	276	7	1	376	290	480
1954	144	6	6	219	200	220
1955	198	5	7	402	210	410
1956	409	65	6	702	480	710
1957	n.a.	n.a.	n.a.	642	460	730
1958	n.a.	n.a.	n.a.	n.a.	670	1,960

SOURCES: From *TGY*, p. 57, and SSB communiqués, various years.

5. Reclamation costs which are not included in basic construction investment

Of the above five items, four are available from our previous tables. "Rural housing construction" is the only item that remains to be estimated. Shigeru Ishikawa has compiled the relevant official data for this estimation; he has also filled in the gaps in the official data. His figures for the value (in millions of yuan) of construction done by private building firms, agricultural cooperatives, individual farmers, and so forth, are presented here:[5]

1952	1,750	1955	2,410
1953	1,430	1956	3,980
1954	2,040	1957	2,940

Of course, these figures include both urban and rural construction. If we can estimate the portion of urban construction in this cate-

5. Shigeru Ishikawa, *National Income and Capital Formation in Mainland China*, pp. 71–72.

gory for each year and subtract it from the total, what is left would be "rural housing construction."

To determine the value of the urban portion we must answer two questions: First, who in the urban areas was allowed to use private builders for construction? Second, what was the total capacity of private builders in the urban areas? The answer to the first question sets an upper limit, and the answer to the second, a lower limit.

Private builders could undertake residential construction outside the state plan, and also nonresidential construction for private or private-state joint enterprises (both industrial and commercial). According to official statistics, total urban housing construction in the period 1953–56 was 66.4 million square meters; of that, 5.4 million square meters were outside the state plan. In addition, no more than 5 per cent of the new urban dwellings were built with private funds.[6] The total amount of housing investment outside the state plan and housing investment financed by private funds in the urban areas during the four-year period is estimated at 440 million yuan. Official sources also revealed that the gross value of fixed assets in private industry dropped from 2,350 million yuan in 1952 to 1,070 million yuan in 1955, whereas the gross value of fixed assets of joint enterprises rose from 640 million yuan to 2,800 million yuan over the same period.[7] For the two types of enterprises combined, the increase in fixed assets between 1952 and 1955 amounted to 880 million yuan. Half of this was probably new construction.[8] New construction of private and joint commercial enterprises in the four-year period was about 700 million yuan. The total amount (residential, industrial, and commercial construction) would then be 1,580 million yuan (440 + 440 + 700).

Actually, a large part of the 1,580 million yuan of construction work was undertaken by state-owned building enterprises. For instance, private-state joint enterprises were strongly inclined to

6. Kang Chao, *The Construction Industry*, p. 96.
7. N. R. Chen, *Chinese Economic Statistics*, p. 147.
8. Although the construction share in total fixed investment was high for the whole economy, it varied drastically according to the type of project. The share could be near 100 per cent for highways, housing, water control, and irrigation projects, but it was ordinarily around 50 per cent for industrial plants.

contract with state-owned building enterprises rather than private builders. Even the private investors in housing projects or individual households had the same preference, because state-owned building enterprises were in a more favorable position than private builders for obtaining building materials which were controlled by the government.

More crucial is the limited capacity of private building firms. The construction industry was in fact one of the few sectors that underwent thorough nationalization in the early years of the Communist regime. The employment of private building firms declined to 18,000 persons, or 1.7 per cent of total employment in the construction industry, as early as 1952.[9] It must have been less than 1 per cent in the subsequent years. The private builders' percentage of output value should be even less than that, because they were smaller in size and poorer in equipment. Therefore, the output value of private builders could hardly have exceeded 50 million yuan per year in the period 1952–57. It is recognized, however, that some residential construction in the urban areas may have been carried out by householders themselves. In view of all these factors and evidence, we may set 10 per cent as the urban portion of Ishikawa's figures. Thus, rural housing construction should be 90 per cent of the values given on p. 102 for each year.

The estimates of rural housing construction so derived, plus the other four items, are presented in table 28. Some of these items are stated in constant prices, whereas others are in current prices. Rural housing construction, reclamation costs, and other imputed investment are based on constant prices. Conceptually, the amounts for water conservation are of a mixed nature, because while the portions of state investment are based on current prices, the underpayments of draft labor have been computed with constant wage rates. Values of implements, carts, and livestock are based on current prices. Since we have no information as to whether their prices had been adjusted by the government in the period, we do not know whether the current prices differ from the constant prices, let alone how to make any necessary adjustments. However, our failure to convert the current prices of those items into constant prices is unlikely to have created any significant margin of error.

9. *TCKTTH*, 1956, No. 24, p. 31.

Table 28

GROSS FIXED INVESTMENT IN THE FARM SECTOR, *1952–57*

(in millions of yuan)

	1952	1953	1954	1955	1956	1957
Rural housing construction	1,575	1,287	1,836	2,169	3,582	2,646
Modern farm implements	0	8	27	116	448	394
Old-type implements, carts, and livestock	842	1,146	1,098	1,139	1,317	1,161
Water conservation	560	540	362	702	1,332	1,266
Other imputed investment	835	848	864	1,053	1,066	1,080
Reclamation	169	140	152	267	331	541
State investment in agriculture, forestry, and meteorology	189	284	156	210	480	460
Totals	4,170	4,253	4,495	5,656	8,556	7,548

SOURCES: Rural housing construction: See the text.

Modern farm implements: For 1953–56 we multiply the "total amounts of means of production supplied to agriculture" (*TGY*, p. 170) by the percentages of purchases of modern farm implements by farmers in various years (Chu Ching, Chu Chung-chien, and Wang Chih-ming, *Reorganization of the Rural Market in Our Country*, p. 41). Since no such percentage is available for 1957, we use 1956's percentage for that year. For 1952 the amount is assumed to be zero.

Old-type implements, carts, and livestock: from table 5.

Water conservation: We add up the figures in column (4) of table 27 and the estimated underpayments of draft labor (Kang Chao, *The Construction Industry*, p. 216). Here it is assumed that draft labor has been used exclusively on water conservation projects.

Other imputed investment: from table A-14.

Reclamation: from table A-12.

State investment in agriculture, forestry, and meteorology: from table 27. The 1957 figure is not officially given, but it is assumed to be identical with the amount in column (5) of the same table.

The sums of various items of gross fixed investment in the farm sector range from 4,170 million yuan in 1952 to 8,556 million yuan in 1956. Because these sums might seem unexpectedly large, we shall make a closer examination of them.

Three of the seven items presented in table 28—water conservation, reclamation, and state investment in agriculture, forestry, and meteorology—are expenditures of the government; they do not represent a direct financial burden on the peasants. Official estimates of farmers' own investment perhaps do not include the item "other imputed investment." As noted earlier, one official source implies the total gross fixed investment by farmers in the whole period of 1953–57 at about 18 billion yuan. If we compute the cumulated total of the first three items in table 28 for 1953–57, we obtain a figure of 18.4 billion yuan, which is surprisingly close to the official estimate.

Of course, the fact that our estimate is close to an official estimate does not necessarily establish the credibility of our estimate. An independent examination is still desirable. Let us convert our totals into per capita of rural population per annum figures and then compare them with some official survey results of the same nature.[10] Since three of our items are government investment, no such comparison is necessary for them. What remain are four items in table 28. In order to put our data and the survey data in comparable classifications, we have combined the two items "modern farm implements" and "old-type implements, carts, and livestock" into one item called "implements, carts, and livestock." The other two items are "rural housing construction" and "other imputed investment."

One official survey report furnishes the information we require for our comparison: "Data from the Representative Survey of the Distribution of Income in 228 Agricultural Cooperatives in 1957," published by the State Statistical Bureau.[11] Since the cooperatives surveyed were located in twenty-four provinces, the geographical coverage of the sample is quite broad. However, it is necessary to point out some important features of the survey findings so far as the investment comparison is concerned. First, the cooperatives in the sample were relatively large in size and better in economic conditions. The results might therefore be somewhat above the true national averages. Second, the investment figures refer only to the assets collectively owned by the cooperatives, but the values have been divided by the total number of member households in order to obtain the "shares" for each member household. In other words, the values of assets are those which appeared on the balance sheets of the cooperatives; no properties still owned privately by individual households are included. For our purpose, this may not create a serious problem in the case of investment in farm

10. The average rural population for the period 1952–57 was 524.95 million. It should be noted that the rural population is not identical to the agricultural population.

11. *TCYC*, 1958, No. 8, pp. 8–12.

implements, carts, and some types of livestock, because a majority of these items had become collectively owned by 1957. But a serious problem does arise for investment in building. The survey report gives only the investment in office buildings, warehouses, and other structures collectively owned by the cooperatives. Yet the bulk of rural housing investment falls into the category of residential houses, which in 1957 were still privately owned. Third, all fixed investment figures in the report are conceptually net of depreciation. For each item of fixed assets, the annual investment has been derived from the difference between the value at the beginning and that at the end of the year, namely, the net increase in value in the year. Fourth, as the article itself emphatically warns the reader, in many cooperatives surveyed the numbers of working days of labor spent on capital creation were seriously underreported.

Our calculations of the average annual fixed investment per capita according to our estimates for 1952–57 and the per capita investment in the official survey for 1957 are as follows:

	Survey data[12]	Our estimates
Rural housing	0.60 yuan	4.15 yuan
Implements, carts, and livestock	2.60 yuan	2.44 yuan
Other imputed investment	2.60 yuan	1.83 yuan
Totals	5.80 yuan	8.42 yuan

We may examine each of the three items individually. The reader may recall that our estimates of "other imputed investment" were originally derived from the information in this sample survey. We have, however, scaled down the magnitudes of this item for the years before 1956 on the ground that labor mobilization in the rural sector was less intensive before the formation of agricultural cooperatives. Consequently, our estimate presented above, as an average for the whole period, is smaller than the survey finding, which refers to 1957 only. Our estimated average for "implements, carts, and livestock," which was derived from the official data on

12. The survey data are originally given as figures per household. The average size of households surveyed was 4.96 persons in 1956 and 5.09 persons in 1957. We use a round figure of five persons per household to convert the original data into per capita figures.

sales of those articles to the rural sector, is slightly lower than the survey finding.

The crucial problem centers on the comparison of rural housing investment. According to the sample survey, the value of housing was 5 yuan per household at the beginning of 1957 and 8 yuan per household at the end of 1957. Therefore, the net investment in housing in the year was 3 yuan per household, or 0.60 yuan per person. However, as we noted, the survey figures include only collectively owned structures. The difference between our estimate of 4.15 yuan and the survey finding of 0.60 yuan represents the per capita gross investment in rural residential housing. The amount is 3.55 yuan per person or 17.75 yuan per family,[13] which is barely enough to cover annual depreciation of housing for each rural family. T. C. Liu has estimated the average value of rural residential housing in 1952 as 749 yuan per household.[14] If the average life-span of rural residential housing is assumed to be forty years, the annual depreciation would be 18.72 yuan per household.

One may suspect that Liu's estimate of the average value of rural residential housing in China is too high, because rural houses are generally poor in quality. But houses of poor quality also have short life-spans. If we assume that, on the average, each person in the rural areas occupies about four square meters of living space or six square meters of construction area, and the construction cost of rural housing is 15 yuan per square meter of construction area, which is only one-fifth of the construction cost of urban apartments or poor residences, the asset value of housing per rural family would then be 450 yuan. If the average life-span of such poor rural houses is assumed to be twenty-five years, the annual depreciation per household would still be 18 yuan. In any case, our estimate of rural housing investment seems quite conservative.

In view of the above comparisons, our estimates of farm investment in fixed capital are not too high at all. The aggregate amounts seem large simply because agriculture is such a predominantly large sector in the economy. Many investment activities in rural China entail labor input only and do not create direct financial

13. The figure includes both cash investment and investment in kind.
14. Ta-chung Liu, "Quantitative Trends in the Economy" in *Economic Trends in Communist China*, ed. A. Eckstein, W. Galenson, and T. C. Liu, p. 171.

burden on peasants. Therefore, these investment activities have often been ignored in studies of Chinese agriculture. Even these semingly enormous amounts of rural investment are believed to have been preponderantly for replacing annual capital consumption in that sector. T. C. Liu has estimated that the total value of reproducible capital stock (excluding land) existing in the farm sector in 1952 was about 95 billion yuan.[15] If an average life-span of thirty years is assumed for the capital stock in that sector, his computation would imply an annual depreciation of 3.17 billion yuan, or total depreciation charges of 19 billion yuan for the whole period of 1952–57.

In his study of capital formation in Communist China, K. C. Yeh has arrived at a figure for total gross investment in the farm sector for the whole period of 1952–57 of 25.26 billion yuan.[16] This is much smaller than our estimate of 34.68 billion yuan for the same period, because he has understated the investment in rural housing.

After a very careful scrutiny of the Chinese Communist statistics, Ishikawa has derived an estimate of total net farm investment in fixed capital in the First Five-Year Plan period (1953–57) of 16.74 billion yuan.[17] Our estimated total of gross fixed investment in the farm sector for the same five-year period is 30.5 billion yuan. If both figures are accepted, the implied proportion of net to gross fixed investment in the farm sector is 54.9 per cent. This is higher than the 40 per cent indicated in an official source.[18] The discrepancy, however, can be explained by the fact that the 40 per cent figure refers to the investment by farmers and cooperatives in housing and implements, which consists of a larger proportion of replacements, whereas Ishikawa's computation includes the government's investment in water conservation and agriculture, which is virtually all new additions to capital stock in the rural sector.

Having established the validity of our estimates of farm investment, we can subtract them from overall fixed investment in each

15. *Ibid.*
16. Yeh, "Capital Formation," in *Economic Trends,* ed. Eckstein, Galenson, and Liu, pp. 511 and 521.
17. Ishikawa, *National Income,* p. 187.
18. *TCYC,* 1958, No. 6, p. 29.

year to derive the gross fixed investment in the nonfarm sectors. As can be seen in table 29, prior to the First Five-Year Plan the farm sector took more than half of the total fixed investment of the economy, but its share was sharply reduced to a range between 32 and 38 per cent in the First Five-Year Plan period.

Table 29

FARM AND NONFARM INVESTMENT IN FIXED CAPITAL, *1952–1957*
(values in millions of yuan)

| | Our estimates | | | | Basic construction within and outside state plans, in nonfarm sectors |
| | Farm | | Nonfarm | | |
	Value	Share (in per cent)	Value	Share (in per cent)	
1952	4,170	51.1	3,983	48.9	3,760
1953	4,253	36.8	7,292	63.2	7,230
1954	4,495	32.4	9,385	67.6	8,650
1955	5,656	36.7	9,777	63.3	8,680
1956	8,556	37.6	14,222	62.4	13,610
1957	7,548	36.2	13,296	63.8	12,640

SOURCES: Our estimates of farm investment: from table 28. Our estimates of nonfarm investment: obtained by subtracting farm investment from total fixed investment given in table 6. Basic construction in nonfarm sectors: data are taken from *TGY*, p. 57. For each year, investment in agriculture, forestry, water conservation, and meteorology is subtracted from total basic construction investment.

Table 29 also compares our estimates with official figures for basic construction investment within and outside state plans in the nonfarm sectors. While the two series for the nonfarm sectors are constructed with entirely different approaches, our estimates may be regarded, conceptually, as the result of adjusting the official series for differences in coverage and valuation basis. Yet the two series are very close in magnitude for all the years. This implies that to a considerable extent our adjustments have canceled each other out. The closeness between the two series gives us the confidence to apply the percentages of sectoral distribution of the official series to our series. The underlying assumption is that whatever net difference between the two series may remain is proportionally distributed among all nonfarm sectors. The results so computed (plus farm investment) are presented in table 30.

Table 30

DISTRIBUTION OF GROSS FIXED INVESTMENT, BY ECONOMIC SECTOR,
1952–57

(in millions of yuan)

	1952	*1953*	*1954*	*1955*	*1956*	*1957*
Farm sector	4,170	4,253	4,495	5,656	8,556	7,548
Industry	1,792	2,858	4,158	4,840	7,125	7,605
Construction	96	365	385	372	683	479
Prospecting for natural resources	76	197	319	284	412	319
Transportation, post, and telecommunication	808	1,079	1,614	1,975	2,731	2,181
Trade	132	277	422	391	782	399
Culture, education, and scientific research	294	627	732	665	1,038	971
Public health and welfare	60	153	169	117	114	133
Urban public utilities	179	248	263	254	370	412
Government administration	20	277	235	156	171	186
Others	526	1,211	1,088	723	796	611
Totals	8,153	11,545	13,880	15,433	22,780	20,844

SOURCES: The table has been constructed through the following steps:
(1) Subtract total farm investment (from table 28) from total fixed investment (from table 6).
(2) Subtract the distribution percentage for agriculture in total basic construction investment (from *TGY*, p. 59) from 100 per cent. Use the remainder to divide all distribution percentages for the 10 nonfarm sectors so that the ten new percentages will add up to 100 per cent.
(3) Use these new percentages to distribute the nonfarm investment obtained in step (1) into the ten nonfarm sectors.

Having obtained these results, we may proceed to compare the shares of investment in industry and in agriculture. It is important to note that the distribution among the nonfarm sectors given in table 30 is based on "functional" rather than "administrative" classifications.[19] The main difference between the two systems of classification is the treatment of housing investment. According

19. *TGY*, p. 59, footnote.

to the administrative classifications, dormitories and residential houses built by a state industrial enterprise, for example, will be treated as part of industrial investment. But according to the functional classifications, all new dormitories and residential houses are lumped together in the item of "other investment," regardless of the nature of investors. To make our comparison meaningful, the estimates of farm investment should be adjusted to exclude rural housing construction too. The resulting comparison is presented in table 31.

Table 31

COMPARISON OF GROSS FIXED INVESTMENT IN AGRICULTURE
AND INDUSTRY, EXCLUDING HOUSING, *1952–57*

	Agriculture		Industry	
	Amount (millions of yuan)	*As percentage of total fixed investment*	*Amount (millions of yuan)*	*As percentage of total fixed investment*
1952	2,595	31.8	1,792	22.0
1953	2,955	25.7	2,858	24.8
1954	2,659	19.2	4,158	30.0
1955	3,487	22.6	4,840	31.4
1956	4,974	21.8	7,125	31.3
1957	4,902	23.5	7,605	36.5

SOURCE: Computed from tables 28 and 30.

The share of industrial investment was smaller than that of agricultural investment in 1952 and 1953 but was larger in the following years. The share of agricultural investment, never falling below 20 per cent except in 1954, was far from insignificant, as some observers have believed. Actually, this finding should not be surprising. In spite of China's energetic drive for industrialization and a heavily concentrated dose of state investment funds in industry, gross fixed investment in agriculture managed to maintain an important position in total fixed investment because agriculture in China has its historical weight. This pattern can hardly be changed in the course of a few years.

To put it in another way, if a country's agricultural sector produces 50 per cent of annual GNP, the country has to spare at least a few per cent of her GNP to make up capital consumption in that sector, so that farm output will be kept from falling in absolute amount. As long as agricultural production largely stays outside the domain of state economic planning, and as long as farm income has not been depressed by the government's extractive policy down to the absolute subsistence level, this investment will naturally take place.

During the First Five-Year Plan period in the Soviet Union, the share of gross fixed investment in industry was 40.9 per cent whereas that in agriculture was 19.2 per cent.[20] This by no means implies that the Soviet Union was more aggressive in her industrialization policy than the Chinese Communists. The really important factor responsible for the difference in investment shares in the two countries is that the Soviet Union had a relatively smaller agricultural sector and a relatively larger industrial sector to begin with.

However, the relative shares of China's industrial investment and agricultural investment will be altered substantially if we measure net investment only. The proportion of net in gross investment in agriculture in that period was lower than the proportion in industrial investment.[21]

At any rate, the true story for 1952–57 is that while agricultural investment began with an historically predominant share, the industrialization drive entailed a far larger proportion of "marginal investment" for industry. This is fully reflected in the rapid rise in the share of industrial investment.

Now let us turn to the allocation of fixed capital investment within the industrial sector. Since the coverage of the official statistics on investment in industry is nearly complete, the percentage distribution of industrial investment among various branches as officially given may be accepted for use. In the First Five-Year Plan the Peking government announced the distribution of basic construction investment among seven industrial ministries, both in absolute amounts and in percentages.[22] These data are, however, not too useful for our purpose, for two reasons. First, they represent the planned targets. By the time the plan was terminated both the

20. K. C. Yeh, "Soviet and Communist Chinese Industrialization Strategies," in *Soviet and Chinese Communism: Similarities and Differences*, ed. D. W. Treadgold, p. 334.
21. See table 31.
22. FFYP, p. 30.

quantities and the percentages had changed. Second, the classification according to industrial ministries has altered frequently. We shall use official statistics published in *TGY*, in which the final accounts of fixed capital investment in industry are broken down between heavy industry (including iron and steel, nonferrous metals, electric power, coal, petroleum, machine-building and metal processing, building materials, and lumber) and light industry (including textiles, food processing, drugs and medical supplies, paper-making, and other light industries).[23] In table 32, we have applied these distribution percentages to our new estimates of industrial investment in various years between 1952 and 1957.

Table 32

DISTRIBUTION OF FIXED CAPITAL INVESTMENT IN THE INDUSTRIAL
SECTOR, BY MAJOR BRANCHES, *1952–57*

	Light industry		*Heavy industry*	
	Investment (millions of yuan)	*Percentage*	*Investment (millions of yuan)*	*Percentage*
1952	431	24.0	1,361	76.0
1953	503	17.6	2,355	82.4
1954	732	17.6	3,426	82.4
1955	596	12.3	4,244	87.7
1956	983	13.8	6,142	86.2
1957	1,156	15.2	6,449	84.8
Average	733		3,996	

SOURCES: The distribution percentages are taken from *TGY*, p. 61. They are then multiplied by the figures in the second line of table 30.

Here the outstanding feature of the Stalinist model of industrialization is clearly manifested. The proportion of investment that went to heavy industry was 76 per cent as early as 1952. Throughout the First Five-Year Plan period (1953–57) it ranged between 82 and 88 per cent; the investment in light industry varied from 12 to 18 per cent of total industrial investment. The average investment in light industry of 733 million yuan per year probably did not leave too much for net capital formation. The total value of

23. *TGY*, p. 61.

fixed assets of industrial enterprises in the whole country in 1952 was officially given at 15.8 billion yuan.[24] If half of this amount was in light industry and if the average life-span of those capital goods was twenty years, then the annual depreciation would have amounted to about 400 million yuan. This must have been the minimum capital consumption of light industry in all likelihood; the actual amount could have been higher.

The dearth of statistical data does not permit us to make similar computations and comparisons for the years after 1957. It is generally believed that the same distribution pattern was carried over to 1958–59, though the percentage (9.9) of basic construction investment (within and outside the state plan) going to agriculture, forestry, water conservation, and meteorology in 1958 was slightly higher than the average percentage (7.6) achieved under the First Five-Year Plan.[25] If the incomplete coverage of the official basic construction investment is adjusted, the share of gross fixed investment in the farm sector in 1958 and 1959 was probably in the range of 30 to 35 per cent.

The reorientation of economic policy came only after the Great Leap Forward had collapsed and the economy had sunk into a serious depression. Many Chinese Communist leaders identified the agricultural sector as the origin of the whole crisis, and a new policy was formulated accordingly. The early 1960's are known as a period of "economic readjustment, consolidation, filling out, and raising standards." The new economic policy was passed at the Ninth Plenary Session of the Eighth Central Committee,[26] and its details were disclosed by Chou En-lai in his report at the National People's Congress in March 1962.[27] The keynote of the policy reversal was to place the highest priority on agricultural production.

The "agriculture first" strategy is clearly manifested in the increase in modern inputs to farm production in the period (see table 33). The supply of chemical fertilizer and the consumption of electric power went up spectacularly. Outputs of farm tractors and power-driven irrigation and drainage equipment reached their

24. *TGY*, p. 93. This figure is based on original purchase prices.
25. *TGY*, p. 59.
26. *JMJP*, Jan. 21, 1968.
27. *JMJP*, April 17, 1962.

peaks in 1960; they then dropped rather drastically in 1961-64, not only because of the general economic crisis but also because of the changed technological policy in farm production.[28] There had been a great debate among the Chinese Communist leaders in the early 1950's over whether China should mechanize farm production in view of the labor surpluses existing in the rural areas. The new leaders who came to power in the early 1960's, after the failure of the Great Leap Forward, were generally opposed to the premature mechanization, on the ground that tractors and many other farm machines would raise labor productivity but not the yields per unit of land. For a special reason, however, they were compelled to continue the tractor production, though at a lower rate. As a result of the Great Leap Forward and the formation of communes, large numbers of draft animals had died from overwork, lack of care, or malnutrition. China urgently needed tractors to replace the lost draft animals, at least as a short-run measure.

More disastrous was the fanatic drive to build irrigation projects during the Great Leap Forward period. The total irrigated area in the country rose from 520 million mou to 1 billion mou in a single year—1958.[29] The new irrigation systems were poorly built and lacked proper design; they caused localized floods, soil salinization, and declines in unit yields of crops. Finally those disastrous irrigation systems had to be abandoned, so that the total irrigated area fell to 480 million mou in 1964.

It is quite obvious that the focus of the new policy to support agriculture in the early 1960's was on current farm inputs rather than capital inputs. This is evidenced by the rapid increase in chemical fertilizer production, as shown in table 33. Chemical fertilizer is capable of raising the productivity of land, which is by far the most scarce factor in China's agriculture.

Therefore, so far as agricultural investment is concerned, in the period 1960-65, the remarkable increases took place in working capital, mainly in the form of government loans to farmers for purchases of chemical fertilizer. In terms of absolute amounts, total rural investment in fixed capital may have declined somewhat as compared with that in 1956-59, because of the cessation of

28. For a fuller discussion see Kang Chao, *Agricultural Production in Communist China 1949-1965,* chaps. 4 and 5.

29. TGY, p. 130.

Table 33

INCREASE IN MODERN INPUTS TO AGRICULTURAL PRODUCTION, 1957–65

	Chemical fertilizer (in 1,000 tons)			Farm tractors (in standard sets)		Power-driven irrigation and drainage equipment (1,000 h.p.)		Electric power consumption in rural areas (million kwh)
	Domestic production (1)	Imports (2)	Total supply (3)	Domestic production	Total stock	Domestic production	Total existing capacity	
1957	871	1,073	1,944	0	24,629	260	560	108
1958	1,462	1,246	2,708	957	45,330	700	1,610	142
1959	2,227	1,078	3,305	5,598	59,000	2,000	3,380	n.a.
1960	2,550	865	3,415	24,800	79,000	2,700	5,900	n.a.
1961	2,000	882	2,882	15,200	90,000	600	4,500	1,000
1962	3,000	991	3,991	14,800	103,400	640	4,000	1,550
1963	4,200	1,789	5,989	17,800	115,000	1,760	6,000	2,100
1964	5,900	1,134	7,034	21,900	123,000	1,400	7,300	2,500
1965	8,900	1,989	10,889	25,000	130,500	1,680	8,570	3,200

SOURCES: From Kang Chao, *Agricultural Production in Communist China*, Madison, 1970.

reclamation and construction of water conservation projects and the reduction of nonstate investment in the rural sector. However, in a relative sense, the share of fixed investment in agriculture must have risen in this period, because the reduction in nonfarm investment was even more serious.

In nonfarm sectors, indications are that fixed investment in transportation and communication, trade, culture and education, public health, and government administration was negligible. Even in the areas of industry and public utilities, investment was highly selective. Judging from scattered reports, the priority order of investment in industry and public utilities seems to have been as follows:

1. On the top of the schedule were defense industries and chemical fertilizer production. The desire of the Chinese Communist leadership to expand rapidly production of nuclear and conventional weapons is understandable. The Sino-Soviet dispute meant not only a removal of the Soviet military shield for China but also some added frontier (the Sino-Soviet borders) to be defended. Furthermore, imports of weapons from the Soviet Union, perhaps from Eastern European countries as well, were cut off. Confronting an increased defense burden and a reduction in outside supply of military goods, China could not but accelerate as quickly as possible her own production of military hardware. Investment in the chemical fertilizer industry was based on the planners' diagnosis of the recent economic crisis and the prescribed remedy.

2. Emphasis was also given to a few extractive industries, especially petroleum, nonferrous metals, and coal. Although the petroleum shortage had long existed in China and was aggravated by the reduced supply from the Soviet Union after the rift between the two countries, investment in this area on a large scale was not feasible until the discovery of the new, rich oil field in Taching in 1959. The expansion in the mining of nonferrous metals was probably stimulated by the rising needs in the defense industries.

3. A considerable amount was invested in production of synthetic fibers, and a crash program of constructing new cotton textile mills was launched in 1965. The former was clearly aimed at lessening the dependence of light industry on agriculture. The crash program in 1965 was probably motivated by a decision to

increase textile products as foreign exchange earners, in view of the quite successful crop of cotton in 1964 and promising prospects in the future.

In summary, although there are fewer concrete data available to us, we can nevertheless conclude that investment in fixed capital during the post-Leap period was not only truncated in size but also allocated to various sectors for a number of reasons that are quite different from the considerations underlying the investment policy in the 1950's. On the whole the attitude of the Chinese Communist government was more cautious; so far as industry and agriculture are concerned, the allocation of state funds for fixed investment was more "balanced" in this later period.

CHAPTER 8

Summary and Conclusions

THE CHINESE official statistics on fixed investment under the Communist regime are both incomplete in coverage and distorted in valuation. Several Western studies have attempted to correct those shortcomings, but none has been sufficiently successful. Our study represents a new approach to the problem.

Instead of making adjustments to the official aggregate data on investment, as other studies have done, we have used the commodity flow method. Estimates have been made for five investment components: construction and installation, domestic production of machinery and equipment, imports of machinery and equipment, office furniture and tools, and other rural investment. The five components have then been combined to form the estimates of total fixed investment. But in using this method we have been able to cover not only the investment made by the government within the state plan of basic construction but also the investment made by private concerns and households outside the state plan. The commodity flow method has also permitted us to adopt a new valuation basis. The biases in the official valuation stemmed from two main sources: the underpayment of work brigades (draft labor) and the peculiar exchange rates used for computing the official values of imported goods. These biases have been removed in our estimates. Following are our resulting estimates of total fixed capital formation in various years (in billions of 1952 yuan):

1952	8.1	1957	20.8	1962	9.4
1953	11.5	1958	35.7	1963	11.6
1954	13.8	1959	43.4	1964	16.7
1955	15.4	1960	39.5	1965	22.3
1956	22.7	1961	17.2		

We have divided our computation into two periods, 1952–57 and 1958–65. While our general method is more or less the same, our estimates for the two periods differ considerably in statistical refinement because of the decreased quantity and poorer quality of the basic data available to us for the latter period.

Our estimates generally confirm the government's claim of investment acceleration in 1952–57. The average annual rate of fixed capital investment, that is, the proportion of GDP devoted to fixed capital formation, was 17.8 per cent in that period. This is remarkably higher than the estimated average rate of 7.5 per cent for 1931–36.[1] If the comparison is made in terms of net capital formation, the difference between the two periods would be even wider. However, the years 1952–57 were followed by a period of tremendous fluctuations in fixed capital investment. Although there are no national income statistics, official or otherwise, which can be used to compute the exact rates of investment, we can say that the rates must have fallen to very low levels in 1961–64.

Thus, one may wonder whether China's experience in 1952–57 was the "normal" result under new economic institutions and policies or just an "exceptional" and "temporary" spurt in investment. After all, the economic history of many industrialized countries is replete with instances of short-run bursts of investment activity. Was the Chinese situation in the 1950's just another such instance? Could the low level of investment in either the 1930's or the early 1960's be regarded as a normal achievement of a low income country? In other words, is the low investment level basically associated with the low level of national income regardless of the economic system under which the nation is operating? Or, in more sophisticated terms, could the ups and downs in investment level in the three periods be "functionally" interrelated? That is to say, could they be just different phases of long-term investment cycles which would continue despite drastic changes in economic institutions?

Admittedly, our study is so limited in temporal scope because of data deficiencies that we can hardly make any conclusive distinc-

1. K. C. Yeh, "Capital Formation," in *Economic Trends*, ed. A. Eckstein, W. Galenson, and T. C. Liu, p. 511. Although the figure includes investment in working capital, 99 per cent of it is for fixed capital investment for the period 1931–36 as a whole.

tion between what is normal and what is exceptional or between a trend and cyclical movements. But in relevant materials other than investment statistics, one will find indications that the performances in prewar China and in the Communist period were basically different. Instead of being independent of economic institutions, the level of investment is a significant function of economic institutions.

As in many underdeveloped countries, the speed of capital formation in prewar China was decisively constrained by the low level of voluntary saving in the private sector. In addition to the low level of income, the extremely low life expectancy gave rise to an age structure of the population unfavorable to saving efforts. An extraordinarily large proportion of people were under the working age. Both the birth rate and the infant mortality rate were high, so that a considerable amount of economic surplus in society had to be wasted on raising children who never grew old enough to participate in productive work.

So far as capital formation is concerned, the main change in the 1950's occurred in the saving mechanism. Instead of relying on voluntary savings, the new government mobilized compulsory savings for the purpose of investment. The traditional constraint on saving was greatly relaxed thereby. In this way, the system of socialist planning can potentially serve as a shortcut to industrialization for underdeveloped countries.

The compulsory savings were realized in two major forms. First, through controls over wages and over prices of consumer goods, and the procurement programs and taxation in the rural areas, the government was able to restrain the consumption level and create budgetary surpluses. Those budgetary surpluses were tailored to, and would be used for, state investment. This is clearly shown by the chief role played by basic construction investment of the government in total capital formation throughout the Communist period.

The second form of compulsory saving was the direct use of surplus labor in rural areas for capital construction, such as road building and large water conservation projects. Although labor conscription is not unique in China, the scale on which the Peking government used it during 1956–59 was certainly unprecedented. This scale would have been impossible had China not been socalized and the rural population not been regimented.

The steadily rising rate of investment in 1952–56 reflected the changed saving mechanism and the new investment drive of the Communist government; it was not the accidental burst of investment that is occasionally observed in a market economy. China really attempted to cut short the industrialization process by socializing the economy. However, compulsory savings in a socialist country are not without limitation. One of the serious problems is the contradiction between work incentives and a high rate of accumulation. As this study has shown, the economic policy of the Peking government entailed a high marginal propensity to invest. If over a long period most of the fruits of capital formation are devoted to further investment, sparing very little for improving living standards, the working masses might feel disappointed. This in fact was a major issue discussed by economists and planners in China in 1956–57.[2] The consensus was that, while the pre-1956 rate of investment was correct, the rate in 1956 might be regarded as excessive. This review of investment policy led to the moderation in 1957.

Unfortunately, all the cautious opinions were silenced by Mao Tse-tung, who believes that revolutionary zeal can effectively overcome physical or material constraints. The Second Five-Year Plan, carefully formulated by planners and formally approved by the National Congress, was torn up by Mao as soon as it was made public. In its place came Mao's Great Leap Forward movement. The fanatic investment and production drives nearly disintegrated the economy. The policy reversal adopted by the new leadership in the early 1960's was meant to salvage the collapsing economy. One of the most urgent tasks was then to shift the emphasis from investment to consumption, so that work incentives could be restored.

What happened in China during the early 1960's must be con-

2. See, for instance, Po I-po, *HHPYK*, 1956, No. 20, p. 72; Li Wei, *TKP*, Dec. 2, 1956; Chu Cheng-ping, *CCYC*, 1957, No. 3, p. 129; Niu Chung-huang, *HH*, 1957, No. 16, p. 440; and Yang Po, *HH*, 1957, No. 20, p. 556. Po I-po's article, entitled "Correctly Handle the Relation between Accumulation and Consumption," explicitly mentions that basic construction increased by 277 per cent in 1953–56 whereas consumption rose by only 29 per cent.

sidered abnormal. It is only in very broad terms that one can connect the ups and downs in investment in the Communist era in a "functional" way. That is, in such a political system there is no way to avoid extremist leaders. Consequently, extremist economic policies may occur from time to time, and policy reversals are required (i.e., functionally related) to redress the biases or heal the wounds.

Another crucial question is: What role did capital formation play in China's economic growth during the Communist period? Interestingly, Western economists have traveled a full circle in their analyses of the function played by investment in an economy. The early Keynesian model, which focused on the problem of short-run stability in an economy, treated investment as a component of effective aggregate demand. This demand component was so volatile in a market economy that its fluctuation tended to cause depressions or inflations if it was not offset by a proper compensatory policy of the government. This view was later modified by E. D. Domar, who emphasized the double role of investment— as a demand component and as a capacity-creating factor on the supply side; from the new thesis came the famous Harrod-Domar model of economic growth. Thereafter, investment became virtually the most important element in all growth models developed by other economists. The importance of investment rested on its capacity-creating nature.

Another sharp turning point in the investment and growth theories came when R. M. Solow built his neoclassical model of economic growth.[3] It is called a neoclassical model because it assumes that full employment prevails all the time. Hence the function of investment as a demand component is completely ignored. The remaining question is then: How important is the other role played by investment—capacity-creating—in economic growth? According to Solow's original calculation based on American historical data, the contribution of investment to economic growth was far less important than that of technological advancement. His results showed that 87 per cent of the increase in output per unit of labor input came from technological progresses and only 13 per cent stemmed from the expansion of capital stock.

3. R. M. Solow, "Technical Change and the Aggregate Production Function," *Review of Economics and Statistics*, No. 39 (1957), pp. 312–320.

One criticism of Solow's initial model was that the measured contribution of technological changes is really a residual which reflects the working of all economic forces other than the inputs of labor and capital. Moreover, the importance of investment is understated because the model assumes that all technological changes have been the disembodied type. Yet in reality the majority of innovations have to be embodied in new machines and equipment; the gains from those innovations cannot be realized unless firms make investments. This last point led Solow to develop his vintage model of economic growth, in which the embodiment effect of investment is taken into consideration.[4] However, even in the vintage model and many other works which have subsequently appeared to refine Solow's theory, the contribution of investment to economic growth is still overshadowed by other factors.

In a sense, in economic theory the importance of investment has shifted back from its connection with long-run economic growth to the connection with short-run economic stability. In other words, investment is important primarily because it is such a vital component in aggregate demand. In an affluent society, investment must take place at a high rate if effective demand is to be maintained at full employment. Otherwise a depression would set in.

In China investment has played a more important role than any that has been envisioned by the above models. Its importance, however, does not lie on the demand side. As a rule, there is no worry about demand deficiency in underdeveloped countries, since the propensity to save is low and there are adequate investment outlets. In fact, many of those countries are under constant pressure from inflation simply because domestic aggregate supply falls short of aggregate demand. In the case of Communist China, the situation is further simplified because the government has full control of saving, consumption, and investment.

The crucial role of investment is on the supply side. But even there the Solow model of economic growth does not apply fully. In view of the enormous gap in technology between China and industrially advanced countries, the proportion of technical changes that are of the embodied type must be greater in China than in the United States. Similarly, the quality difference of capital goods

---

4. R. M. Solow, "Technical Progress, Capital Formation, and Economic Growth," *American Economic Review* 52 (May 1962):76–78.

between two successive vintage points must be much wider in China than Solow's model has postulated.[5]

More important is the fact that Solow's neoclassical assumption of full employment does not hold in China at all. China is perhaps the country with the largest surplus population, that is, persons whose marginal productivity falls below the minimum subsistence cost. In prewar China, capitalist firms hired workers up to the point at which their marginal productivity was equal to the subsistence wage. Thus, the bulk of surplus labor existed in the rural communities, where peasants, whether landowners or tenants, shared their incomes among family members. The situation has not drastically changed in the Communist era, since even state enterprises are unlikely to hire workers at a cost much higher than their contributions to production.

The marginal productivity of surplus labor is so low because the existing stock of capital goods is not sufficient to match the labor force. Only investment can provide extra employment opportunities in the urban areas and absorb unused labor productively in the rural areas. Therefore, in a backward country, both the technological changes and the absorption of surplus labor into production require new investment for embodiment. Where the amount of surplus labor is exceedingly large, as it is in China, the absorption of unused labor outweighs the embodiment of technological changes as the primary source of economic growth. In other words, output is increased at a higher speed by putting the unused labor in production rather than by raising the productivity of those who are already employed.

Unfortunately, there is a conflict between the embodiment of technical changes and the absorption of unused labor. The new machines and production techniques developed by the advanced countries, including the Soviet Union, tend to be labor-saving, because their economies are characterized by labor shortages. Direct borrowing of modern technology from those countries without any adaptation would provide a minimum opportunity for new employment per unit of investment funds. This conflict is clearly demonstrated by the Chinese experience in their First Five-Year Plan.

5. In his vintage model Solow assumes a 5 per cent annual increase in the quality of capital goods. *Ibid.,* p. 78.

More than 80 per cent of the investment within the state plan in the First Five-Year Plan period went to heavy industry. It is estimated that investment in large plants accounted for over 60 per cent of the planned total investment in industry.[6] Ordinarily those large modern plants would require a relatively small amount of labor inputs per unit of fixed capital. In September 1956, when Chou En-lai announced the final version of the First Five-Year Plan, he anticipated that the industrial enterprises newly constructed or reconstructed during 1953–57 would contribute 15 per cent to the gross industrial value product for that period.[7] By the end of 1957, however, it turned out that those new enterprises had actually contributed about 30 per cent to the gross value product.[8] This increase was made possible through some adaptations to intensify the use of labor, such as the larger number of shifts of workers to assure a twenty-four-hour operation of machinery and equipment.

Even a 30 per cent output increase was low compared with the amount of investment. According to official statistics, fixed assets of industrial enterprises increased by 123 per cent between 1952 and 1957, while the numbers of industrial workers increased as follows:[9]

	Number *(in 1,000 persons)*	*Index* *(1952 = 100)*
1952	4,939	100
1953	6,188	125.3
1954	6,408	129.7
1955	6,477	131.1
1956	8,626	174.7
1957	9,008	182.4

In view of the preponderance of large-scale construction units in the investment plan, the average gestation period must have been more than one year. Therefore, the increase in industrial employment in 1953 must have been due to the rehabilitation work in the previous years. This also explains why industrial employment re-

6. Chao, "Policies and Performance in Industry," in *Economic Trends*, p. 570.
7. *FFYP*, p. 39.
8. Lin I-fu, "Seek All Effective Means to Develop Fully the Productive Potential in Existing Industrial Enterprises," *CHCC*, 1958, No. 3, p. 12.
9. *TGY*, pp. 93, 183. The employment data do not include apprentices.

mained almost constant in 1953–55 despite the investment activities in those years. The net addition to employment due to new investment under the First Five-Year Plan was less than three million or about 30 per cent of the total number of industrial workers in 1957. The drastic rise in the marginal capital-labor ratio in that sector is obvious.

Even the three million additional jobs could not have been created without the help of some labor-using adaptations. Attempts were made in this period to apply the system of multiple shifts to more and more enterprises, old and new. In several mining industries a system of four overlapping shifts, each of eight working hours, was introduced for the purpose of avoiding the slowdown of operation during the changing of shifts.

The planners soon realized the limited function of investment in creating employment opportunities. Opinions were expressed in 1957 against the so-called gigantism in industrialization and in favor of small plants and labor-intensive methods of production. Undoubtedly, the Walking with Two Legs policy of 1958–59 was a direct outcome of this debate. The new policy was nothing but a planned dualism in industrial technology, which redefined the investment criteria.

These changes in technology in industry may be seen from the following indicators:[10]

	Unit	1952	1957	1958
Consumption of electricity per worker	kwh	1,430	2,606	942
Capacity of power machinery per worker	hp	1.73	3.01	1.25
Fixed assets per worker	yuan	3,525	5,168	2,026

More dramatic was the sudden burst in the number of industrial workers—from 9 million in 1957 to 25.6 million in 1958.[11]

Although the new direction was certainly correct, the reorientation was carried out to such an extreme extent as to endanger the whole economic structure. In fact, this was partially responsible for

10. Chao, "Policies and Performance in Industry," in *Economic Trends*, p. 572.
11. *TGY*, p. 183.

the subsequent economic crisis. The indigenous production units that mushroomed in 1958–59 produced only goods of excessively poor quality at prohibitively high costs; some items turned out by those firms were virtually useless. The government was soon compelled to abandon most of those indigenous production units. The investment policy adopted by the new leadership during 1961–65 was essentially a middle road, so far as the technological choice is concerned. It attempted to avoid the extreme in either direction. Although emphasis continued to be given to small-scale plants, those units were required to meet certain efficiency standards. Only under these circumstances could capital formation be expected to make its maximum contribution to economic growth.

We may conclude from our study that the Chinese experience has clearly demonstrated both the merits and demerits of the Communist approach to capital formation. On the credit side, a planned economy with all means of production controlled by the government can easily break some of the formidable barriers to economic growth that are generally encountered by underdeveloped countries. On the debit side, such an economy has no automatic mechanism which can effectively prevent economic policy in general and investment policy in particular from going to the extremes. The resulting series of adjustments and counteradjustments are a highly costly process.

APPENDIX A

Official Definitions of Investment Components

THE BEST WAY to eliminate confusion is to begin by itemizing the accounts of basic construction, for which it is possible to identify the coverage from official documents.

I. Basic construction within the state plan (國家計劃内基本建設). This category is close to, but not identical with, "public investment in physical capital," as used by some Western economists. It is a measurement gross of depreciation but net of "major repairs." One thing which has been overlooked by most students of Communist China is that the scope of the state plan for basic construction underwent some enlargement in 1957. Before that year, the state plan included only activities carried out by enterprises and business organizations directly subordinate to the central government. It was enlarged in 1957 to embrace activities conducted by the administration and miiltary organizations of the central government and fourteen types of enterprises and organizations belonging to various levels of local government.[1] The following are the items included in basic construction:

A. Construction work (建築工程).[2] This covers the erec-

1. There were also other minor changes. See *CHCC*, 1957, No. 5, p. 30.
2. The definitions of basic construction components, with varying degree in detail, can be found in *CHCC*, 1957, No. 5, pp. 29–33, and No. 6, pp. 28–30; *TCKT*, 1957, No. 8, pp. 14–16; *TCKTTH*, 1956, No. 13, pp. 30–33; *JPRS*, 1957, June 19, 1963, pp. 1–5; *FFYP*, p. 23; *KJJP*, Nov. 27, 1962; and *FKHP*, 1953, pp. 297–301.

tion of new buildings, fixed structures, and public utilities together with service facilities which become integral parts of the buildings and structures and are essential to their use for any general purpose, and the restoration and alteration of existing buildings and structures. Structures include dams, reservoirs, canals, docks, mines, refineries, highways, airfields, bridges, railways, etc. Utilities include power transmission and distribution lines, petroleum pipe-lines, telephone and telegraph lines, water supply lines and sewers, etc. Examples of service facilities included in construction are plumbing, heating and lighting equipment, sanitation fixtures, elevators, etc. Construction also includes the task of demolishing existing structures or obstacles for construction purposes, clearing land, landscaping, and the placing and fostering of perennial plants.[3] But it does not include any "major repair" or "minor repair" of existing buildings and structures. "Major repairs" will be entered in item (III B). This category also excludes all small construction projects below a given value,[4] which are subsumed as "minor fixed assets"—see item (III C).

B. Installation of equipment and machinery (安裝工程).
C. Purchase of machinery, equipment, work tools, and testing instruments (購買設備工具和儀器). The value of equipment which must be installed in whole or in part on a constructed foundation or frame before it can be put into operation will be included in the current basic construction investment only when it has been completely installed.[5] Otherwise its value will be treated as "inventories." For work tools, instruments, and equipment which do not have to be mounted on a fixed foundation or frame, the full value will be counted as soon as they are delivered to the constructing unit.[6]

3. This refers to the plants surrounding a new building only. The general activity of forestation is treated as accumulation for working capital. See *TCKT*, No. 19, p. 18.
4. *CHCC*, 1957, No. 5, p. 30. The exact dividing line in value terms is not given.
5. *TCKTTH*, 1956, No. 13, p. 32.
6. *Idem.*

D. Ancillary expenses of basic construction (直接為基建工程 服務的費用項目). Most items included here do not fall into the category of investment according to the Western concept. They are, however, treated as part of basic construction investment in the statistical practice of Communist China. This category consists of the following:

1. Expenses for the purchase of housing, other structures, and draft animals. This type of expense does not represent an addition of capital goods for the society as a whole. It is associated with transfers of properties.

2. Expenses of land acquisition and compensation for people who are removed from the acquired land. This item is particularly important for water conservation and hydroelectric power station projects. For instance, more than half of the total investment in the San Men Hsia hydroelectric power station project was spent for this purpose.[7]

3. Expenses for cadre training. This compromises expenses for the training of technicians to meet production requirements.

4. Expenses of geological prospecting, surveying, and architectural designing. The scope of this item has undergone drastic change. Before 1955, costs of all resource geological prospecting, engineering geological survey, and architectural designing were counted in basic construction investment. Beginning in 1955, all these expenses, with only a few minor exceptions,[8] were no longer included; since then this item has practically been eliminated, and two new accounts have been

7. SLFT, 1957, No. 1, p. 7.
8. The changed regulation is cited in CHCC, 1957, No. 5, p. 30; TCKT, 1957, No. 8, p. 14; and CHCC, 1957, No. 7, p. 32. According to 1955's new regulation, there are six exceptional cases in which the costs of prospecting and designing will be included in basic construction investment. None of the six cases is very important. However, in the registration of values of assets in an enterprise, which is separate from the statistical reports of basic construction, the costs of engineering geological surveys and architectural designing should be allocated to and included in the values of various assets (see TCKTTH, 1956, No. 13, p. 32). This practice is primarily for the purpose of determining a proper amount of annual depreciation of assets in an enterprise.

created outside the category of basic construction. See items (II A) and (II B).

5. Other expenses. These include expenses incurred by an organization when its plants are moved to another location, expenses for disposing of suspended projects, and other administrative expenses of the constructing unit.

II. Government expenses related to but not included in basic construction investment (與基建有關的其他政府支出).[9]

There are the following components under this heading:

A. Geological prospecting (地質勘探). This includes both resource geological prospecting and engineering geological prospecting.

B. Surveys and designing (勘察設計). Both I (A) and II (B) were included in basic construction investment before 1955.

C. Equipment reserves (器材儲備). This is an item set in the First Five-Year Plan for equipment reserved for use after 1958.

D. Cash reserves (準備金).

E. Expenses of reclamation to be performed by armed forces (軍墾費).

III. Other government capital outlays (政府其他投資).

A. Working capital (流動資金). This is for the purpose of carrying inventories in state enterprises. However, the appropriation for this category each year should not be identified with the total increment in inventories, or what is called investment in inventories in the West, of state enterprises in that year. In addition to the government budget appropriation, state enterprises often borrow from the state banks for the purpose of increasing inventories; on the other hand, state enterprises may use the working capital appropriation to repay these bank loans.[10] More-

9. FFYP, p. 23.

10. For instance, the central government appropriated 1.68 billion yuan to state enterprises as working capital in 1955 but instructed individual enterprises to use these funds solely to liquidate their borrowing from the state banks. Consequently, this working capital appropriation did not result in any increase in inventories in state enterprises. See the state budget report of 1955, JMST, 1957, pp. 162–163.

over, some key materials and commodities are held as "state reserves" under the Bureau of State Reserves of Materials (which was merged with the Bureau of Material Supply in 1956).[11] The state reserves, though not held by individual enterprises as part of their inventories, should nevertheless be treated as inventories in the ordinary sense when the country is taken as a whole.

B. Major repairs (大修理). This category has been singled out from basic construction, and the disbursement for major repairs in state enterprises comes from the major repair fund which is part of the total depreciation charge of state enterprises.[12] A distinction is also made between "major repairs" and "minor and medium repairs"; the latter are treated as activities not of the construction industry but of service industries. However, the term "major repair" itself is only loosely defined as the replacement or repair "on a large scale" of the worn-out parts or components of a building or a structure in order to "restore its use value." Reroofing and replacing a new heating system in a house have been cited as examples. It is not clear how a demarcation line is actually drawn between "major repairs" and "minor and medium repairs."

C. Purchase of minor fixed assets and construction of small projects (零星固定資產購置). Funds for these purchases and projects come from the central government appropriation. For administrative reasons they are not subject to the normal procedures for controlling basic construction funds and accordingly are excluded from the category of basic construction. The establishment of this account has created confusion, and its integration into basic construction has been strongly suggested.[13]

D. Maintenance costs of public utilities (公用事業維護費).

E. Costs of trial production of new products (產品試製費).

F. Other expenditures (其他費用).

11. See *JMJP*, Oct. 27, 1955, and *HHPYK*, 1956, No. 11, p. 5.
12. *TCKTTH*, 1956, No. 1, p. 31.
13. *CHCC*, 1957, No. 5, p. 30.

The aforementioned items are investment activities and related expenditures of the government within the state plan. In the proposal of the First Five-Year Plan and annual state budget reports one will find that three terms have been employed with differing coverage: "basic construction investment," which is confined to category I; "basic construction investment and related expenditures," covering categories I and II;[14] and "economic construction expenditures," [15] embracing categories I, II, and III.

It should be noted that basic construction investment is not identical with the term "volume of basic construction completed." The former embraces all investment work done in place, whereas the latter term refers to the "completed" portions. Specifically, when the whole construction project is completed, it is called a "completed project." For a large project, when an independent unit is finished before the completion of the whole project, this portion is called "finished work" on an "unfinished project"; and there is "unfinished work" on an "unfinished project." While all the three categories are included in "basic construction investment," only the first two categories are counted in the "volume of basic construction completed." The two magnitudes are equal only when the volume of "unfinished work" remains the same at the beginning and the end of the year.

Some investment activities involve no appropriation from the state budget. However, the scope of "basic construction investment outside the state plan" is not entirely clear. Judging from the term itself, it should comprise all investments in fixed capital made by units with their own funds (that is, not appropriated by the state budgets). One article specifies the following items as excluded from the state plan:[16]

1. Investment financed by labor unions and cooperatives
2. Investment financed by the state-private joint enterprises through their own earnings

14. In *FFYP* (p. 23), it is called "total investment in basic construction" to indicate its broader coverage than "basic construction investment."
15. See the State Budget Reports of various years.
16. *CHCC*, 1957, No. 5, p. 30.

3. Investment financed by state enterprises through their bonuses or welfare funds
4. Certain construction projects of local governments, such as primary schools built by the governments below the hsien level

However, this article does not give an exhaustive list of items of investment outside the state plan, and it fails to explain whether investment made by private firms and individual farmers is part of investment outside the state plan. Other Chinese sources indicate that investment outside the state plan does include the construction activities of peasant members of agricultural cooperatives and individual farmers.[17]

In addition to the above terms and the already too complicated classification, the Chinese statistical authorities have used several other concepts which are across-the-board terms and again vary in coverage.

The term with the broadest coverage is "accumulation." Of all the terms used by the Chinese Communist economists, this is the one which is closest to the Western concept of net domestic investment. Specifically, accumulation in a given year consists of the following:[18]

17. TCKT, 1957, No. 8, p. 16.
18. TCYC, 1958, No. 5, pp. 16–21. There are different interpretations by Western scholars of the Chinese Communist definition of "accumulation." According to Yueh Wei, an economist in the Chinese State Statistical Bureau in charge of national income accounts, accumulation is defined as additions to productive and nonproductive fixed assets and increases in working capital and stockpiling. Examples of productive fixed assets are factory buildings, mineshafts, blast furnaces, dikes, power equipment, lathes and metal working equipment, tools and apparatus, various production implements, means of transportation, and draft animals; examples of nonproductive fixed assets are residential houses, government buildings, schools, hospitals, clubs, and nurseries. CCYC, 1956, No. 3, p. 63. The definition and examples clearly show that this term is a comprehensive concept of net investment. However, in their book *The Economy of the Chinese Mainland: National Income and Economic Development 1933–1959*, Liu and Yeh have a different interpretation of the term "accumulation." While accepting Yueh Wei's definition (p. 230), they insist that it has omitted services or contributions rendered by passenger transportation and financial organizations in connection

1. Basic construction investment within the state plan but exclusive of ancillary expenses, that is, including items (IA), (IB), and (IC) only
2. Increases in inventories of state enterprises and government organizations [not identical with item (IIIA)] and increases in state reserves of materials
3. Purchase of minor fixed assets and small construction projects
4. Increases in weapons of the armed forces
5. Investment outside the state plan, in both physical capital and working capital
6. Minus annual depreciation.

Another term used by the Chinese planners is "new fixed assets," which is equivalent to the Western concept of gross investment in physical capital. According to the provisions effective before 1956, anything worth more than 500 yuan and having a normal life-span of more than one year was considered a fixed asset.[19] The minimum value was lowered in 1956, however, to only 200 yuan.[20] Included in "new fixed assets" are:[21]

1. Basic construction investment within the state plan, exclusive of ancillary expenses
2. Purchase of minor fixed assets and small construction projects—item (III C)
3. Fixed assets not in current use, that is, as inventories or state reserves

with investment (p. 235). This contention is difficult to justify. As Yueh Wei points out, the Chinese national income and accumulation accounts have been separately compiled. Data for the latter are taken from various annual statistical and accounting reports and survey results concerning changes in fixed assets, working capital, and material reserves. It is extremely unlikely that the State Statistical Bureau has estimated the value of services rendered by passenger transportation and financial organization in connection with investment and then deducted it from the total value of increases in fixed assets, working capital, and material reserves.

19. Things below the value limit or lasting less than one year are classified as "low value or perishable articles."
20. KYTC, p. 35.
21. Ibid., p. 242.

4. Increases in livestock[22]

5. Investment in physical capital outside the state plan.[23]

22. Only mature animals are counted as fixed assets. Young animals are classified as working capital. See *TCKT*, 1957, No. 19, p. 18.

23. In publishing data, the Chinese Communists usually make a distinction between new fixed assets added within the state plan and those outside the state plan. See, for example, *TGY*, p. 64.

APPENDIX B

The Sino-Soviet
Exchange Rates

THE EXCHANGE RATE SYSTEM of Communist China is extremely complex, not only because it is a multiple-rate system (especially true with the yuan-ruble rates), but also because the exchange rates between yuan and various foreign currencies are inconsistent in relation to each other. Furthermore, there is some indication that for many years in the 1950's, China and the Soviet Union quarreled about the conversion rates of their currencies. Consequently, both countries avoided quoting any yuan-ruble exchange rate in their openly published financial bulletins. Until April 1961, the foreign exchange bulletins of the State Bank of the USSR quoted exchange rates with all foreign currencies except the yuan. The open quotations of the yuan-ruble rates appeared in the Chinese publications at about the same time.[1] To understand the exchange rate system between yuan and the ruble in the 1950's one has to piece together information from scattered sources; some points about its operation in that period are still quite obscure.

According to an internal directive of the People's Bank of China issued on January 29, 1957, there existed by then three different official yuan-ruble (old) rates:[2] 0.50 yuan to the ruble, 0.80 yuan to the ruble, 0.95 yuan to the ruble. Another internal directive of

1. *Shih-chieh chi-hsi nien-chien,* 1961 (World Knowledge Yearbook, 1961) (Peking, World Knowledge Publishing House), p. 1323.
2. Directive of the People's Bank of China, January 29, 1957, Number Yin-Kuo-Tsai 25, in *FKHP,* 1957, p. 59.

the People's Bank of China issued on December 18, 1959, instructed all its branches: "At the close of business on 31 December, all ruble accounts should be converted to jen min pi at the rate of 0.1667, 0.50, 0.80, or 0.95." [3] Clearly, there then existed four yuan-ruble rates, that is, the new rate of 0.1667 yuan to the ruble had been added to the above three rates.

The rate of 0.95 yuan to the ruble was a so-called trade ruble rate,[4] which became effective probably sometime in April 1950. Since China's trade with Eastern European Communist countries was stated in rubles too, this trade ruble rate was applicable to trade transactions with "new democratic countries" as well. Chinese publications have used this rate to compute the costs of imported machinery.[5]

However, neither Soviet nor Eastern European sources have ever mentioned the exchange rate of 0.95 yuan to the ruble.[6] This should not be surprising, because this rate was virtually useless for countries other than China. When the Soviet Union or any European Communist country traded with China, both imports and exports were priced and recorded in rubles. Since the Chinese currency unit never entered into her foreign trade accounts, there was no need to use the yuan-ruble rate.

The rate of 0.80 yuan to the ruble has appeared only in the two directives we cited above. The directives did not make clear to what categories of transactions the 0.80 yuan rate applied. Nor do we know the effective date of this rate. However, there is no doubt

3. "Notice on Foreign Exchange Adjustments of Transactions in Rubles," issued by the Head Office of the People's Bank of China, December 18, 1959, Number Yin-kuo-tsai 400, in *JPRS*, 19499, May 31, 1963, pp. 137–139.

4. See Yeh Chi-chuang's speech, *HHPYK*, No. 16, 1957, p. 93.

5. For instance see *JMTY*, 1958, No. 1, p. 14. Comparisons of the yuan figures and ruble figures of Sino-Soviet trade in the 1950's also imply a conversion rate of about 1 to 1. See Alexander Eckstein, "Sino-Soviet Economic Relations—A Reappraisal," in *The Economic Development of China and Japan*, ed. C. D. Cowan p. 146; and Kang Chao "Pitfalls in the Use of China's Foreign Trade Statistics."

6. One Soviet source, however, mentions a yuan-ruble rate of 1 to 1 prior to 1960. See I. P. Aizenberg, *Valintnaia Sistema SSSR* (Moscow, 1962), p. 149. Unfortunately, while the author cites the data sources for other exchange rates he has tabulated in his book, he fails to cite the source for the yuan rate. I suspect that he obtained this rate by comparing Sino-Soviet trade figures.

that this rate was another "trade ruble" rate parallel to the 0.95 yuan rate. The December 18, 1959, directive called both the 0.95 and the 0.80 yuan rate "trade ruble" rates, and instructed the branch offices on how to convert the accounts in those trade ruble rates into "adjusted trade rubles." Presumably, the 0.80 yuan rate applied to a special trade category, much narrower in the scope of application than the 0.95 yuan rate.

The rate of 0.50 yuan to the ruble was undoubtedly a nontrade rate,[7] and it seems to have been the center of dispute between the two countries so far as the issue of exchange rates is concerned.[8] The Chinese maintained a strict distinction between foreign trade transactions and nontrade transactions and used different exchange rates. Nontrade transactions included the expenses of delegations to foreign countries, diplomats, students going abroad, and other exchanged personnel.[9] The trade ruble rate had very little real meaning other than for bookkeeping purposes. Whether China gained or lost in her trade with the USSR depended on her bargaining power in setting the ruble prices for her imports and exports. Once those ruble prices and the total trade volume in rubles were determined, the exchange rate that would be used to convert the ruble figures into yuan was immaterial. However, the nontrade rate was more significant in a real sense. It would determine the real purchasing power of one country's currency in the other country, for example, how many Chinese goods a Soviet diplomat stationed in China could buy with his monthly salary. That is why the nontrade rate became a point of dispute between China and the USSR when there was no objective way to determine a rate acceptable to both countries.

Unlike the trade ruble rate, which had been pegged for about ten years, the nontrade rate underwent many changes. The first nontrade rate was set on June 1, 1951, at the level of 6,754 old yuan

7. For instance, *CHKY*, No. 10, 1957, p. 5, states: "The cost of designing performed in the Soviet Union required 4,000 rubles per person per month; this amount is equal to 2,000 yuan." Since no ruble-yuan exchange could apply to both trade and nontrade transactions, the 0.5 yuan rate implied by the above statement must be a nontrade rate.

8. See Iu. V. Vladimirov, "The Question of Soviet-Chinese Economic Relations in 1950–1966," in *Chinese Economic Studies* 3, no. 1 (1969): 24.

9. See *FKHP*, 1957, p. 59.

to the ruble.[10] This rate was meant to be temporary, and the two countries agreed that it should be discontinued when China had completed her monetary reform and established a gold content for her currency. However, the rate was adjusted on September 22, 1953, even before China carried out her monetary reform.[11] This time, the rate was set at 5,000 old yuan to the ruble. The Chinese monetary reform finally came in March 1955, with the new yuan equivalent to 10,000 old yuan. However, the Soviet government did not agree to readjust the nontrade rate between the yuan and the ruble, probably on the ground that the Chinese monetary reform failed to set a gold content for her new currency unit; the nontrade rate was simply put at 0.5 yuan to the ruble. China's dissatisfaction with this rate is quite noticeable; many publications refused to recognize it as an official rate.[12]

China had been for a long time aware of the fact that the nontrade rate of 0.5 yuan to the ruble, or 2 rubles to the yuan, greatly undervalued the yuan. Yet the Soviet government refused to adjust the rate because the yuan had no gold content to "tell" its exact "value." In early 1957 the Eastern European countries took concerted action to set new nontrade exchange rates between their currencies and the Soviet ruble. These countries selected a standard market basket of about seventy-five commodities and services to compute purchasing power parities between their currencies and the Soviet ruble. Those parities then became the new nontrade exchange rates. The action of the Eastern European countries gave China a good excuse to reopen the old issue. China finally persuaded the Soviet Union to sign a protocol on December 30, 1957, by which the ruble value of the Chinese yuan was appreciated by 200 per cent in the nontrade rate.

The new rate is said to have been "established on the basis of prices in the CPR for representative industrial and food commodities and on the basis of prices for services as compared with prices for similar goods and services in the USSR." [13] Whether they were the same standard market basket used by the Eastern

10. See Iu. V. Vladimirov, *op. cit.*, p. 22.
11. *Ibid.*
12. *Hsueh-shu yueh-kan* (Academic Monthly), No. 10, 1957, p. 55; *Chi-hua ching-chi* (Planned Economy), No. 12, 1957, p. 29.
13. Iu. V. Vladimirov, *op. cit.*, p. 24.

European Communist countries is not clear. The new rate was 0.1667 yuan to the ruble or 6 rubles to the yuan. However, two things should be noted. First, the Soviet authorities were rather reluctant to accept this adjustment. Instead of calling this adjustment a 200 per cent appreciation of the yuan, they called it an imposition of a 200 per cent surtax on ruble payments for non-commercial transactions.[14] Second, the original nontrade rate of 0.5 yuan to the ruble was not abolished. Therefore, there existed two parallel nontrade rates between January 1, 1958, and January 1, 1960. This should be very clear from the 1959 directive of the People's Bank of China cited earlier. Furthermore, the scope of application for the rate of 0.1667 yuan to the ruble was much smaller.[15]

China continued to bargain with the Soviet Union on this point until a new Currency Agreement was reached by the two countries on December 15, 1959.[16] It was based on this agreement that the People's Bank of China issued the directive which we cited earlier. The directive contains the following statement:

The State Council has issued directives (59) Yin-mi-kuo-ching-1295, *Beginning 1960 All Settlements in Trade Rubles with Socialist Countries Will Be Changed to Adjusted Trade Rubles, and Scope of Application of the Adjusted Rate.*

Regarding unadjusted pre-January 1, 1960, settlements, the Ministry of Finance has agreed to make up the difference to the bank. Therefore, a check should be made of 1959 foreign exchange settlements.

Any trade settlements made at the unadjusted rate should be recalculated at the adjusted rate and entered in the Foreign Exchange Buying and Selling Account, and the differential in the Funds Receivable Account or Funds Payable Account.[17]

The directive then goes on to give some numerical examples showing how the trade ruble accounts should be adjusted. The 0.95 yuan rate and the 0.80 yuan rate are referred to as unadjusted trade ruble rates, whereas the 0.50 yuan rate is called the adjusted trade ruble rate. It is therefore very clear that, according to the new agreement, the two original trade ruble rates were abolished,

14. *Ibid.*
15. See M. K. Klochko, *Soviet Scientist in Red China*, p. 57.
16. *JMJP*, December 15, 1959.
17. *JPRS*, 19499, May 31, 1963, pp. 137–39.

the nontrade rate of 0.50 yuan was made the sole trade rate, and the 0.1667 yuan rate was left as the sole nontrade rate, all effective January 1, 1960.

When the Soviet Union revalued her ruble on January 1, 1961, the remaining two yuan-ruble rates were changed to: 2.22 yuan = 1 new ruble (trade rate); 1.667 yuan = 1 new ruble (nontrade rate).[18] On April 4, 1963, the nontrade rate was once more changed, to 1.29 yuan to the ruble; the trade rate remained the same.[19]

18. See *Shih-chieh chi-hsi nien-chien* 1961, p. 1323, and Iu. V. Vladimirov, *op. cit.*, p. 24.
19. See *Shih-shih shou-tse* (Handbook on Current Events) (Peking, 1965), No. 3, pp. 37–38.

APPENDIX C

Statistics and
Estimation Procedures

Table A-1

CONSTRUCTION INPUTS, PRICES OF INPUTS, AND INDEX, *1950–58*

	Steel (1,000 tons)	Timber (1,000 m³)	Cement (1,000 tons)	Plate glass (1,000 m²)	Other building materials (million of yuan)	Regular construction workers (1,000 persons)	Work brigades (million of man-days)	Input index
1950	120	1,612	1,272	15,600	51.8	400	188	34.7
1951	249	3,449	2,246	18,068	115.6	600	255	61.1
1952	462	4,007	2,417	21,320	338.5	1,050	498	100.0
1953	956	6,418	3,500	24,305	550.2	1,655	359	154.2
1954	1,139	11,843	4,252	31,353	548.8	1,940	310	196.3
1955	1,326	10,857	4,031	27,716	582.8	1,909	652	210.1
1956	2,496	13,458	5,799	30,750	896.7	2,400	1,369	326.2
1957	1,861	12,100	6,080	51,776	946.4	2,283	1,357	292.1
1958	3,255	15,665	8,115	52,670	1,648.6	2,950	3,519	485.1
1952 Price (yuan per unit)	1,270	129	75.44	3.13		569.80	0.80	

SOURCES: From Kang Chao, *The Construction Industry in Communist China*, tables 1, A-7, and A-8.

Table A-2

OUTPUT OF CIVILIAN MACHINERY, 1952–57

Item	Unit	Price	1952	1953	1954	1955	1956	1957
Internal combustion engines	1,000 hp.	320.60/hp	27.6	21.0	26.2	356.7	540.8	609.0
Transformers	1,000 kva	36.86/kva	1,167.1	1,960.7	1,960.7	1,926.0	2,891.1	2,610.0
Steam boilers	ton	27,400.00/ton	1,222	3,223	3,353	2,059	3,022	2,734
Hydroelectric turbines	1,000 kw	500.00/kw	6.7	17.0	25.3	33.4	102.7	74.9
AC electric motors	1,000 kw	155.85/kw	638.7	918.0	947.0	606.9	1,069.0	1,455.0
AC generators	1,000 kw	945.45/kw	29.7	59.0	54.8	107.6	288.3	312.2
Spindles	1,000	364.00/unit	383.1	287.4	489.0	304.4	784.0	484.0
Looms	1,000	1,550.00/unit	6.5	9.7	15.1	9.3	19.3	10.4
Locomotives	unit	257,300.00/unit	20	10	52	98	184	167
Freight cars	unit	21,480.00/unit	5,792	4,500	5,446	9,258	7,122	7,300
Passenger cars	unit	42,680.00/unit	6	30	64	108	311	350
Double-wheel and blade plows	1,000 sets	61.50/set	5.1	3.0	60.5	528.0	1,793.2	689.0
Seeders	set	2,000.00/set	344	4,590	12,469	24,533	74,299	35,350
Metal-cutting machines	ton	2,703.00/ton	13,038	19,231	18,210	15,682	29,662	32,032
Merchant vessels	dw ton	3,323.00/dwt	16,000	35,000	62,000	120,000	104,000	54,000
Bicycles	1,000	142.50/unit	80.0	165.0	298.0	335.0	640.5	806.0
Adding machines	set	270.00/unit	25	263	1,500	2,424	5,060	6,950
Typewriters	set	70.00/unit	1,556	2,188	3,077	4,328	6,086	8,560
Overall output index			100.00	133.44	175.59	231.94	362.96	307.71

Sources: Kang Chao, The Rate and Pattern of Industrial Growth in Communist China, tables C-1 and C-9; and Chu-yuan Cheng, The Machine-Building Industry in Mainland China, chapter 6, tables 1 and 2.

Table A-3

OUTPUT OF CIVILIAN MACHINERY, *1957–65*

Item	Unit	(yuan) Unit price	1957	1958
Automobiles	unit	17,000	7,500	16,000
Metal-cutting machine tools	ton	4,400	40,040	59,000
Power generating equipment	kw	610	198,000	800,000
Power irrigation equipment	Horsepower	220	260,000	700,000
Locomotives	unit	223,850	167	350
Shipbuilding	ton (dead weight)	2,890	54,000	90,000
Tractors	unit	17,200		957
Spindles	unit	317	450,000	1,000,000
Looms	unit	1,350	11,800	15,000
Bicycles	unit	150	806,000	1,174,000
Overall output index			100.00	213.90

SOURCES: Except for those indicated below, data are taken from Chu-yuan Cheng, *The Machine-Building Industry in Mainland China*, chapter 7, table 7.

Automobiles: (1959) *JPRS*, 13052, March 12, 1962; (1963) *CKHW*, Aug. 28, 1964; (1964) *NCNA*, Sept. 23, 1964.

Powered irrigation equipment: (1958) According to *JMJP* (Jan. 14, 1961), a total of 5.4 million h.p. were produced in 1958–60. 1958's output is derived by subtracting from this figure the known quantities of output for 1959 and 1960; (1959) *PR*, Aug. 9, 1960, p. 17; (1960) *KTTH*, 1961, No. 16, p. 20; (1961) *KJJP* (Jan. 18, 1962) states that total output of this item in 1960 and 1961 was 3.3 million h.p.; 1961's output is derived therefrom; (1962 and 1963) estimated from the following information: (a) Total output in 1961–63 was 3 million h.p. (*CKHW*, Aug. 14, 1964), hence 2.4 million h.p. were produced in 1962–63; (b) There was a notable upturn in production of this item in 1963. Output in the first half of 1963 was reported to be 100 per cent

Table A-3 (Continued)

1959	1960	1961	1962	1963	1964	1965
17,700	20,000	10,000	8,500	22,500	27,750	28,400
82,600	74,340	42,900	28,600	37,180	45,760	68,640
1,800,000	2,300,000	1,200,000	1,100,000	1,267,000	1,580,000	1,738,000
2,000,000	2,700,000	600,000	640,000	1,760,000	1,400,000	1,680,000
650	800	180	160	200	350	403
122,300	200,000	60,000	50,000	80,000	100,000	120,000
5,598	24,800	15,200	14,800	17,800	21,900	25,000
1,360,000	600,000	400,000	300,000	500,000	700,000	1,400,000
21,100	12,300	8,200	6,200	10,000	14,000	28,000
1,500,000	1,850,000	980,000	800,000	1,080,000	1,250,000	1,500,000
364.79	453.82	207.71	182.33	274.71	326.55	396.85

higher than that of the corresponding period in 1962 (*PR*, Aug. 2, 1963, p. 16). In the first eight months, the increase in output was 175 per cent (*PR*, Oct. 4, 1963, p. 18). We take 175 per cent as the rate of increase for the whole year of 1963; (1964) total current output is estimated as the increment of existing capacity in that year plus 100,000 h.p. as replacements for worn-out equipment; (1965) estimated by using a 20 per cent rate of increase, which is slightly lower than the rate of increase given in *PR* (Sept. 24, 1965) for the first half of 1965.

Locomotives: (1959) Kang Chao, *The Rate and Pattern of Industrial Growth in Communist China*, p. 128; (1960) *CFCP*, March 21, 1961.

Tractors: (1959) *JMJP*, April 11, 1960; (1960) *KTTH*, 1961, No. 16, p. 20; (1961) *KJJP*, Jan. 18, 1962; (1962) *CKHW*, Sept. 13, 1963; (1963) *CKHW*, Aug. 14, 1964; (1964) *NCNA*, Sept. 26, 1964.

Table A-4

IMPORTS OF MACHINERY AND EQUIPMENT FROM NON-COMMUNIST
COUNTRIES, *1951–65*

	Imports of machinery and equipment (million dollars) (1)	Exports of machinery and equipment (million dollars) (2)	Net imports of machinery and equipment (million dollars) (3)	Net imports, valued c.i.f. (million dollars) (4)	Net imports, valued c.i.f. (million yuan) (5)	Total costs to final users (million yuan) (6)
1951	42.3	0.3	42.0	42.8	236.9	252.3
1952	12.0	0.1	11.9	12.1	67.0	71.4
1953	20.9	0.1	20.8	21.2	117.3	124.9
1954	12.6	0.1	12.5	12.8	70.8	75.4
1955	13.4	1.5	11.9	12.1	67.0	71.4
1956	41.2	2.5	38.7	39.5	218.6	232.8
1957	71.7	2.9	68.8	70.2	388.5	413.8
1958	62.5	7.3	55.2	56.3	311.6	338.1
1959	62.2	9.8	52.4	53.4	295.5	320.6
1960	53.0	5.4	47.6	48.6	267.0	289.7
1961	26.0	5.2	20.8	21.2	117.3	127.3
1962	16.9	5.2	11.7	11.9	65.9	71.5
1963	25.5	10.6	14.9	15.2	84.1	91.2
1964	67.1	10.2	56.9	58.0	321.0	348.3
1965	172.9	19.8	153.1	156.2	864.4	937.9

SOURCES AND EXPLANATORY NOTES: For columns (1) and (2), data are taken from U.S. Mutual Defense Assistance Control Act Administration, *Report to Congress*, various years. The data include the values of machinery, transport equipment, and professional and scientific instruments. However, the following items of parts and consumer durables have been subtracted: ball and roller bearings; insulated wire and cable; tubes, photo-cells, and semiconductors; valves, parts, chassis, flashlight batteries, flashlight bulbs, bulbs, electric fans, radio parts, electric appliances, sewing machines, bicycle parts. The data are at current prices f.o.b. No adjustment is made to eliminate reexports of these countries. The exports to China reported by some countries include goods shipped to North Korea, North Vietnam, Outer Mongolia, or Taiwan.

Column (3) represents the differences between columns (1) and (2). For column (4), a 2 per cent mark-up is added to figures in column (3) to convert them into c.i.f. values. The 2 per cent estimate of seaborne transportation costs and insurance costs is based on the information given in Carmellah Moneta, "The Estimation of Transportation Costs in International Trade," *Journal of Political Economy*, February, 1959, pp. 41–58. To arrive at the figures in yuan in column (5), a computed purchasing power parity of 5.534 yuan to the dollar for machinery and equipment is used. In column (6), the total costs to final users are the figures in column (5) plus 3 per cent for service charges and 3.5 per cent for domestic transportation costs for 1951–57. The rate of service charges is raised to 5 per cent for 1958–65.

Table A-5
IMPORTS OF MACHINERY AND EQUIPMENT
FROM THE USSR, *1950–65*

	Total imports of machinery and equipment, including parts (million old rubles) (1)	Total imports of machinery and equipment, excluding parts (million old rubls) (2)	Total exports of machinery and equipment (million old rubles) (3)	Net Imports of machinery and equipment, excluding parts (million old rubles) (4)	Net imports of machinery and equipment, excluding parts (million yuan) (5)	Total costs to final users (million yuan) (6)
1950	166.0	157.7	0	157.7	96.2	102.5
1951	438.4	416.4	0	416.4	254.0	270.5
1952	647.2	614.8	5.6	609.2	371.6	395.8
1953	644.4	612.2	12.0	600.2	366.1	389.9
1954	795.6	755.8	21.2	734.6	448.1	477.2
1955	924.4	866.0	41.2	824.8	503.1	535.8
1956	1,219.6	1,180.0	36.8	1,143.2	697.4	742.7
1957	1,086.0	1,030.4	25.6	1,004.8	612.9	652.7
1958	1,270.4	1,218.4	17.2	1,201.2	732.7	795.0
1959	2,391.2	2,321.2	49.6	2,271.6	1,386.0	1,503.8
1960	2,016.2	1,930.5	2.9	1,927.6	1,176.1	1,276.1
1961	432.8	397.7	1.2	396.5	241.9	262.5
1962	110.7	75.1	34.8	40.3	24.6	26.7
1963	168.0	119.1	27.6	91.5	55.8	60.5
1964	230.2	195.5	23.1	172.4	105.2	114.1
1965	308.0	282.6	0	282.6	172.4	187.1

SOURCES AND EXPLANATORY NOTES: The data for 1955–1959 in columns (1), (2), and (3) are taken directly from: USSR, Ministry of Foreign Trade, *Vneshniaia Torgovlia SSR za 1955–59. Godi: Statistichesku Sbornik* (The Foreign Trade of the USSR for 1955–59: A Statistical Compilation) (Moscow, 1961), pp. 474–505; the same title for 1959–63 (Moscow, 1965), pp. 374–386; the same title for 1964 (Moscow, 1965), pp. 228–233; the same title for 1966 (Moscow, 1967), pp. 257–262. Instead of using new rubles, we have restored all the data to values in old rubles.

For 1950–54 in column (1), data are taken from Alexander Eckstein, "Sino-Soviet Economic Relations: A Re-Appraisal," in *The Economic Development of China and Japan*, ed. C. D. Cowan, p. 146.

For 1950–54 in column (2), we have used the following estimation procedures. There are separately listed items of parts:

Original code	Commodity
12522	Rollers
18007	Tractor spare parts
18168	Spare parts for farm machinery
19113	Motor vehicle spare parts

Table A-5 (Continued)

The proportion of these four items in total imports of machinery and equipment by China ranged from 2.9 per cent to 6.3 per cent in 1955–60. The average for the whole six-year period was 4.3 per cent. It rose to 30 per cent after 1960, reflecting the desire of China to produce relatively more machinery domestically with foreign parts and unfinished products. We use 5 per cent as an estimate of the proportion of imported parts in total imports of machinery and equipment from the USSR in 1950–54, to be subtracted from the figures in column (1) for those years.

There was only one item of Chinese exports of machinery and equipment, namely, ships (Russian code 192). An examination shows that the values of ships exported from China to the Soviet Union in 1955–59 are closely related to the Chinese production of merchant vessels. By utilizing this correlation we extrapolate the figures for Chinese exports of machinery and equipment to the USSR in 1950–54 in column (3). Chinese production figures of merchant vessels are given in Kang Chao, *The Rate and Pattern of Industrial Growth in Communist China*, pp. 122 and 128. The two sets of data are presented below (figures in parentheses are estimates):

	Shipbuilding in China (in 1,000 dwt tons)	Value of ships exported to the USSR (in millions old rubles)
1950	0	(0)
1951	0	(0)
1952	16	(5.6)
1953	35	(12.0)
1954	62	(21.0)
1955	120	41.2
1956	104	36.8
1957	54	25.6
1958	90	17.2
1959	120	49.6

Column (4) represents the differences between columns (2) and (3). A conversion rate of 1.639 rubles to one yuan is used to convert column (4) into column (5). Figures in column (5) are the yuan values of the Soviet goods delivered at the Sino-Soviet border, inclusive of the transportation costs incurred up to that point. The yuan value figures for 1950–57 are boosted by 6.5 per cent, namely, 3 per cent for service charges and 3.5 per cent for domestic transportation costs within Chinese territory; and the yuan value figures for 1958–65 are boosted by 8.5 per cent because service charges were raised to 5 per cent after 1957. The final results are presented in column (6).

Table A-7

TOTAL IMPORTS OF MACHINERY AND EQUIPMENT
FROM EASTERN EUROPEAN COUNTRIES

	Index	*Value (in millions of old rubles)*
1952		97.6
1953	100.0	371.6
1954	89.1	331.1
1955	106.8	396.9
1956	126.6	470.4
1957	103.6	385.0
1958	277.2	1,030.1
1959	255.5	949.4
1960	268.9	999.2
1961	158.6	589.4
1962	59.9	222.6
1963	33.7	125.2
1964	33.8	125.6
1965	66.9	248.6

SOURCES AND EXPLANATORY NOTES: The index numbers are from table A-6. They are based on selected items of machinery exports to China from those countries, as officially published. The coverage is of course incomplete. We must find the total value of exports of machinery and equipment to China from those countries in any single year in the period and then convert all the index numbers into full values. 1953 is the year that we have found for this purpose. We know the combined total of exports from the Eastern European countries in 1953 from the statistical handbooks published by those countries. The share of machinery and equipment in this total is given by a Chinese official source as 51 per cent (*HHPYK*, No. 9, 1953, pp. 166–167). This source also mentions that the total value of machinery and equipment imported from the Eastern European countries increased by nearly three times from 1952 to 1953. Using the share given for 1953, we can derive the value of machinery and equipment imported from those countries in 1953 as 371.6 million old rubles. The quantity is then divided by 3.8 (i.e., nearly 400 per cent) to get the value of machinery and equipment imported in 1952.

Table A-6

SELECTED ITEMS OF IMPORTS OF MACHINERY AND EQUIPMENT

FROM EASTERN EUROPEAN COUNTRIES

(in 1,000 old rubles)

Country and item	1953	1954	1955	1956
Poland				
Equipment for metal working	9,333	6,662	2,120	6,877
High pressure boilers	0	0	0	0
Excavators and road-building equipment	0	0	0	0
Complete plants	0	0	0	0
Automobiles	0	0	5,592	4,463
Ambulances	0	0	0	0
Ships	0	0	22,480	34,889
Tractors	0	0	1,888	11,227
Combines	0	0	0	0
Surveying equipment	0	0	0	0
Trucks	0	0	0	0
Locomotives	2,414	0	0	0
Hungary				
Thermal power stations	0	0	4,940	2,315
Carrier equipment	393	4,624	10,549	14,647
Trucks	12,190	20,649	15,688	9,688
Tractors	6,072	1,188	2,640	8,085
Lathes	10,534	3,108	495	1,940
Combines	7,772	1,632	3,386	3,529
Buses	17,748	15,453	9,741	4,692
Czechoslovakia				
Excavators			10,224	5,538
Metal-working machines			20,516	13,248
Diesel motors			794	496
Electric motors	48,669	51,676	1	38
Tread tractors			0	13,537
Wheeled tractors			5,075	4,277
Trucks			9,498	7,780
Buses			0	92

1957	1958	1959	1960	1961	1962	1963	1964	1965
6,206	21,793	11,063	2,257	1,073	0	280	243	1,409
0	0	8,568	4,368	0	0	0	0	2,965
9,800	900	3,600	6,100	1,900	100	0	0	711
0	0	81,317	94,775	70,655	42,710	11,049	761	1,771
37	3,233	2,141	3,291	546	27	1,528	5,271	8,902
0	0	0	0	0	0	0	459	2,880
22,841	25,477	0	0	0	1,506	14,447	15,618	14,942
4,138	12,131	2,350	3,359	3,247	0	733	3,720	1,800
0	0	0	0	0	0	0	1,076	0
0	0	0	0	243	405	0	63	261
0	0	21	4,166	0	0	0	0	0
0	1,846	11,218	15,336	0	0	0	0	0
9,502	25,713	15,495	23,233	38,392	1,831	0	0	0
9,820	9,687	14,768	10,485	2,400	668	0	0	0
3,795	13,568	2,820	2,629	1,802	0	0	0	1,897
6,758	5,874	6,402	6,745	5,630	970	0	0	0
4,316	6,772	2,198	139	0	0	0	0	2,000
3,468	224	0	0	0	0	0	0	0
612	0	0	0	0	0	0	0	0
9,585	6,177	4,260	1,917	2,130	0	0	852	426
20,102	73,922	67,269						27,094
136	73,334	20,596						
19	421	47	135,668	42,233	14,833	11,544	11,544	
7,508	10,742	69						10,848
1,993	18,275	20,064						
890	8,215	9,667						
0	4,140	5,888						

Table A-6 (*Continued*)

Country and Item	1953	1954	1955	1956
Bulgaria				
Lathes	2,978	443	0	0
Stationary diesel engines	0	0	0	0
Electric motors	418	0	10	940
Power transformers	0	0	0	0
Pumps	0	0	0	0
Complete plants	0	0	0	0
Tractor-drawn plows	0	77	496	352
Tractor-drawn seeders	0	44	400	1,390
Total value	118,521	105,556	126,533	150,040
Index	100.0	89.1	106.8	126.6

SOURCES AND EXPLANATORY NOTES: Basic data are taken from the following sources: for Poland, *Rocznik Statystyczny*, Glowny Urzad Statystyozny, various years; for Hungary, *Statistical Yearbook*, Kospoti Statisztikai Hivatal, various years; for Czechoslovakia, *Statisticka Rocenka CSSR*, Ustredni Komise Lidove Kontroly a Statistiky, various years; for Bulgaria, *Staticticheski Godishnik na Narodna Republika Bulgaria*, Tsentralno Statistichesko Upravlenie of Bulgaria, various years.

The data are presented in the original sources in four ways: (1) Some series are given in both quantities and values. (2) Some series are given in values only. (3) For some series, both quantities and values are given for a few years, but only quantities are available for other years. (4) Some series are expressed in quantities only for all years. In order to combine all these series and construct index numbers we need value weights—either prices or unit values of the products. For the first two categories of data, there is no problem at all. For the third type of information, we can compute unit values from the years for which both quantities and values are given and apply the unit values so derived to other years where only quantities are available. For the last category of data, to be itemized below, unit values are computed or borrowed from foreign sources.

Item		Source of unit value
Poland:	Locomotives	Poland-USSR trade, from the Soviet Foreign Trade Handbook
Hungary:	Trucks	Poland-China trade
	Tractors	Poland-China trade
	Lathes	Hungary-USSR trade, from the Soviet Foreign Trade Handbook
	Combines	Same
	Buses	Same
Czechoslovakia:	Wheeled tractors	Poland-China trade
	All other items	Czechoslovakia-USSR trade, from the Soviet Foreign Trade Handbook

1957	1958	1959	1960	1961	1962	1963	1964	1965
0	819	1,018	10	765	0	0	0	0
0	476	939	1,390	1,810	1,383	0	0	0
1,252	3,488	1,873	526	683	0	0	0	00
0	476	1,121	1,014	171	154	398	424	1,353
0	402	213	430	2,107	0	5	3	45
0	705	7,854	850	12,147	6,369	0	0	0
0	0	0	0	0	0	0	0	0
0	0	0	0	0	0	0	0	0
122,778	328,548	302,839	318,688	187,934	70,956	39,984	40,034	79,304
103.6	277.2	255.5	268.9	158.6	59.9	33.7	33.8	66.9

It should be noted that Czechoslovakia has published export breakdowns by commodity only for 1955–59. We compute the ratio of the value of all listed items to the total Czech exports to China in 1955 and apply this ratio to Czech exports to China in 1953 and 1954. The results are two lump sums for these two years. In a similar manner, we compute the ratio of the value of all listed items to total exports in 1959 and then apply this ratio to total exports in 1960–65.

All values in national currencies are converted into old trade rubles at the following exchange rates:

Poland:	1 zloty	= 1 ruble
Hungary:	2.935 ft	= 1 ruble
Czechoslovakia:	1.8 crown	= 1 ruble
Bulgaria:	1.7 leva	= 1 ruble (1953–59)
	0.29 leva	= 1 ruble (1960–65)

The above official exchange rates are taken from Kang Chao and Feng-hwa Mah, "A Study of the Ruble-Yuan Exchange Rate," in C. M. Li, *Industrial Development in Communist China*, p. 197, table 1; and People's Bank of China, *Handbook of Various National Currencies*, rev. ed. (Peking: The Financial and Economic Publishing House, 1963), pp. 101–109.

Table A-8

ESTIMATES OF CHINA'S EXPORTS OF MACHINERY AND EQUIPMENT
TO ASIAN COMMUNIST COUNTRIES, *1952–65*

(in millions of old rubles)

	China's total economic aid to Asian Communist countries	China's exports of machinery and equipment to Asian Communist countries
1952	n.a.	0
1953	n.a.	0
1954	200	80
1955	400	160
1956	440	176
1957	440	176
1958	295	118
1959	300	120
1960	260	104
1961	260	104
1962	230	92
1963	230	92
1964	230	92
1965	130	52

SOURCES AND EXPLANATORY NOTES: It may be safe to assume that Communist China has never imported machinery and equipment from Asian Communist countries. However, piecemeal information does indicate that China exported machinery in considerable quantities to these countries every year in the late 1950's; unfortunately, there are no trade statistics with commodity breakdowns available to us. All we can do is to make some crude estimates from the amounts of the Chinese economic aid to these countries (North Korea, North Vietnam, and Outer Mongolia). It is assumed that China's exports of machinery and equipment to the Asian Communist countries were closely related to China's economic aid to them. (Although China granted economic assistance to North Korea even before 1954, we do not include values for those years because we believe that the grants prior to 1954 were military in nature, on the grounds that the Korean war was going on in those years and that China was not capable of exporting machinery at that time.)

Data on China's economic loans to Asian Communist countries are taken from Alexander Eckstein, *Communist China's Economic Growth and Foreign Trade,* pp. 162 and 306. They are converted into values in old rubles. It is difficult, however, to determine the precise quantities of China's exports of machinery and equipment to the Asian Communist countries from the figures for total economic aid. The economic aid figures are very likely to have included costs of consumer goods and technical assistance. Our estimates are derived by applying a 40 per cent allowance to the annual loan commitments. As indicated by an independent test that we have conducted (see p. 72 in the text), China's exports of machinery and equipment to the Asian Communist countries in various years appear to have been based on contractual commitments, so that the quantities maintained a remarkable stability despite China's domestic economic fluctuations. Moreover, that test yields a set of

Table A-8 (Continued)

new estimates of exports of machinery and equipment to those countries, which are surprisingly close to the estimates here. Even if one does not accept that test and believes that the arbitrary 40 per cent may depart considerably from the actual percentage (which we are unable to ascertain anyway), the net effect on our estimates of fixed capital formation would still be negligible. For instance, to reduce the percentage from 40 per cent to zero (that is, to assume no exports of capital goods to those countries at all) alters the estimated magnitude of capital formation by only a fraction of one percentage point.

Table A-9

NET IMPORTS OF MACHINERY AND EQUIPMENT FROM COMMUNIST COUNTRIES OTHER THAN THE USSR, *1952–65*

| | Imports of machinery and equipment from Eastern European countries (millions of old rubles) (1) | Exports of machinery and equipment to Asian Communist countries (millions of old rubles) (2) | Net imports of machinery and equipment from Communist countries other than the USSR | | Total costs to final users (millions of yuan) (5) |
			(millions of old rubles) (3)	(millions of yuan) (4)	
1952	97.6	0	97.6	53.7	57.2
1953	371.6	0	371.6	204.4	217.7
1954	331.1	80.0	251.1	138.0	147.0
1955	396.9	160.0	235.9	130.2	138.7
1956	470.4	176.0	294.0	161.8	172.3
1957	385.0	176.0	209.0	114.8	122.3
1958	1,030.1	118.0	912.1	501.2	543.8
1959	949.4	120.0	829.4	455.7	494.9
1960	999.2	104.0	895.2	491.9	533.7
1961	589.4	104.0	485.4	266.7	289.4
1962	222.6	92.0	130.6	71.8	77.9
1963	125.2	92.0	33.2	18.2	19.7
1964	125.6	92.0	33.6	18.5	20.1
1965	248.6	52.0	196.6	108.0	117.2

SOURCES AND EXPLANATORY NOTES: Columns: (1) from table A-7; (2) from table A-8; (3) differences between column (1) and column (2). (4) based on a price comparison, a conversion rate of 1.82 old rubles to one yuan is derived, and it is used to convert data in column (3) into those in column (4). The yuan values so converted include 10 per cent addition for transportation costs via Russian territory before reaching the Chinese border; (5) derived by adding 6.5 per cent for service charges and domestic transportation costs for 1952–57, and 8.5 per cent for 1958–65, to the data in column (4).

Table A-10

PRICE COMPARISON OF SOVIET AND CHINESE MACHINERY
(price in yuan)

Original serial number	Type of machine	Price of Chinese product	Price of Soviet product	Price ratio
1.	General lathe	4,400	7,400	1.682
3.	Heavy lathe	5,000	6,100	1.220
4.	Hexagon lathe	10,000	14,000	1.400
5.	Single shaft automatic lathe	10,000	14,000	1.400
7.	Multiple chisel semiautomatic lathe	5,700	8,300	1.456
10.	Erect lathe	3,800	4,600	1.211
12.	Erect drilling lathe	4,200	6,900	1.643
13.	Arm-swinging drilling lathe	4,000	4,500	1.125
14.	Multiple shift drill	5,300	8,000	1.509
15.	Reclining warding lathe	5,000	5,150	1.030
17.	Round grinding machine	3,800	6,400	1.684
18.	Internal round grinding machine	5,500	9,600	1.745
19.	Crooked-shaft convex wheel grinding machine	4,000	5,400	1.350
20.	Plane grinding machine	4,000	6,100	1.525
21.	Shaftless grinding machine	5,600	6,400	1.143
24.	Polish and grinding machine	10,700	7,700	0.720
25.	Knife and cutlery grinding machine	5,700	7,700	1.351
26.	Knife and cutlery grinding machine	8,000	17,000	2.125
27.	Teeth wheel	5,300	6,500	1.226
28.	Screwing cutting machine	9,000	13,000	1.444
29.	Horizontal boring	6,000	7,400	1.233
30.	Vertical boring	6,900	7,900	1.145
31.	All-purpose chiseling machine	7,400	9,000	1.216
32.	Lungmen planer	5,700	6,000	1.053
33.	Shaping mill	8,200	20,600	2.512
34.	Chiseling machine	8,200	8,200	1.000
35.	Lungmen planer	3,100	4,400	1.419
37.	Sawing machine	4,500	6,900	1.533
38.	Reaming machine	3,160	6,600	2.089

Original serial number	Type of machine	Price of Chinese product	Price of Soviet product	Price ratio
39.	Pipe cutting and shaping machine	7,500	9,500	1.267
40.	Sawing machine	3,300	4,700	1.424
Average				1.415

SOURCE AND EXPLANATORY NOTES: The data are taken from the Railway Special Services, Design Institute of the Ministry of Railways, People's Republic of China, *Tieh-lu piao-chun she-chi yu-suan shou-tse* (Standard Railway Design and Budget Handbook) (Peking: People's Publishing Housing, 1960), translated in *JPRS* 10913, Oct. 31, 1961, pp. 24–26.

All prices are original (factory) prices exclusive of any transportation expense. The Soviet prices have been converted into yuan in this handbook according to the official ruble-yuan trade rate prevailing prior to 1960.

Table A-11

PRICE COMPARISON OF CHINESE AND EAST GERMAN
AND CZECHOSLOVAKIAN MACHINERY
(price in yuan)

Original serial number	Type of machine	Price of Chinese product	Price of East German or Czecho-slovak product	Price ratio
East German				
1.	General lathe	4,400	6,800	1.545
3.	Heavy lathe	5,000	7,500	1.500
4.	Hexagon lathe	10,000	14,300	1.430
5.	Single shaft automatic lathe	10,000	2,000	2.000
10.	Erect lathe	3,800	5,800	1.526
12.	Erect drilling lathe	4,200	4,900	1.167
13.	Arm-swinging drilling lathe	4,000	3,800	0.950
14.	Multiple shaft drill	5,300	7,800	1.472
15.	Reclining warding lathe	5,000	3,600	0.720
17.	Round grinding machine	3,800	7,600	2.000
18.	Internal round grinding machine	5,500	11,400	2.073
19.	Crooked-shaft convex wheel grinding machine	4,000	5,900	1.475
20.	Plane grinding machine	4,000	6,300	1.575
21.	Shaftless grinding machine	5,600	13,000	2.231
24.	Polish and grinding machine	10,700	11,500	1.075
25.	Knife and cutlery grinding machine	5,700	11,900	2.088
27.	Teeth wheel	5,300	11,200	2.113
28.	Screwing cutting machine	9,000	7,500	0.833
29.	Horizontal boring	6,000	7,400	1.233
30.	Vertical boring	6,900	7,700	1.116
31.	All-purpose chiseling machine	7,400	7,400	1.000
32.	Lungmen planer	5,700	5,400	0.947
33.	Shaping mill	8,200	21,100	2.573
34.	Chiseling machine	8,200	7,100	0.866
35.	Lungmen planer	3,100	3,600	1.161
37.	Sawing machine	4,500	9,000	2.000
38.	Reaming machine	3,160	4,400	1.392
40.	Sawing machine	3,300	6,400	1.939

Table A-11 (Continued)

Original serial number	Type of machine	Price of Chinese product	Price of East German or Czechoslovak product	Price ratio
Czechoslovak				
1.	General lathe	4,400	7,800	1.773
3.	Heavy lathe	5,000	6,100	1.220
4.	Hexagon lathe	10,000	10,200	1.020
5.	Single shaft automatic lathe	10,000	22,000	2.200
10.	Erect lathe	3,800	6,300	1.658
12.	Erect drilling lathe	4,200	9,100	2.167
13.	Arm-swinging drilling lathe	4,000	4,100	1.025
14.	Multiple shaft drill	5,300	7,900	1.491
15.	Reclining warding lathe	5,000	6,100	1.220
17.	Round grinding machine	3,800	7,900	2.079
19.	Crooked-shaft convex wheel grinding machine	4,000	5,600	1.400
20.	Plane grinding machine	4,000	4,300	1.075
21.	Shaftless grinding machine	5,600	10,600	1.893
25.	Knife and cutlery grinding machine	5,700	11,700	2.053
27.	Teeth wheel	5,300	12,300	2.321
28.	Screwing cutting machine	9,000	8,500	0.944
29.	Horizontal boring	6,000	16,300	3.681
30.	Vertical boring	6,900	9,900	1.435
31.	All-purpose chiseling machine	7,400	12,200	1.649
32.	Lungmen planer	5,700	7,300	1.281
33.	Shaping mill	8,200	14,000	1.707
35.	Lungmen planer	3,100	5,500	1.774
38.	Reaming machine	3,160	4,300	1.361
Average				1.579

SOURCE AND EXPLANATORY NOTES: Same as for table A-10.

Table A-12
RECLAMATION INVESTMENT, *1950–65*

Year	Area reclaimed (1,000 mou)	Investment (millions of yuan)
1950	236	14
1951	646	39
1952	2,808	169
1953	2,330	140
1954	2,539	152
1955	4,450	267
1956	5,521	331
1957	9,013	541
1958	18,000	1,080
1959	10,000	600
1960	0	0
1961	0	0
1962	0	0
1963	0	0
1964	0	0
1965	20,000	1,200

SOURCES: Area reclaimed in the years: (1950–57) from Kang Chao, *Agricultural Production in Communist China*, chapter 8; (1958) *CKNK*, 1959, No. 1, p. 12; (1959) *CKNK*, 1959, No. 20, p. 1; (1960–64) total area of cultivated land of state farms and livestock farms did not increase from 1959 to 1964. In 1959 the figure was 48 million mou (*CKNK*, 1959, No. 20, p. 1); in 1964 the figure was 36.5 million mou (*JMJP*, Sept. 19, 1964). The 1964 figure was actually smaller, because some state and livestock farms had been merged into neighboring communes prior to 1964. Since total cultivated land did not increase, we assume that reclamation activities were discontinued in these years; (1965) *Mir sotsializmavtsifrakh i faktakh 1965 god* (Moscow), p. 76.

Investment: The number of mou reclaimed times 60 yuan. For explanations see chapter 3.

Table A-13

PURCHASES OF OLD-TYPE FARM IMPLEMENTS, CARTS,

AND LIVESTOCK, *1952–57*

(values in millions of yuan)

	Total amount of means of production supplied to agriculture (1)	Old-type implements, carts, and livestock as a percentage of (1) (2)	Value of old-type implements, carts, and livestock supplied to agriculture (3)
1952	1,410	59.7	842
1953	1,920	59.7	1,146
1954	2,500	43.9	1,098
1955	2,820	40.4	1,139
1956	3,700	35.6	1,317
1957	3,260	35.6	1,161

SOURCES AND EXPLANATORY NOTES: Columns: (1) from *TGY*, p. 170; (2) A percentage distribution of various categories of producer goods supplied to agriculture in each year of 1953–56 is furnished in Chu Ching, Chu Chung-chien, and Wang Chih-ming, *Wo-kuo nung-tsun shih-chang ti kai-tsu* (Reorganization of the Rural Market in Our Country) (Peking: Financial and Economic Publishing House, 1957), p. 41. We have combined the original items "old-type farm implements" and "other producer goods." The second item consists of livestock, carts, and "producer goods for subsidiary works." Since information is missing for 1952 and 1957, we use 1953's share for 1952, and 1956's share for 1957; (3) column (1) multiplied by column (2).

Table A-14

IMPUTED RURAL INVESTMENT, *1952–57*

	Rural population (×1,000 persons)	Imputed investment (millions of yuan)
1952	503,190	835
1953	510,290	848
1954	520,170	864
1955	531,800	1,053
1956	538,650	1,066
1957	545,650	1,080

SOURCES AND EXPLANATORY NOTES: The data on the rural population are taken from J. S. Aird, *The Size, Composition, and Growth of the Population of Mainland China*, U.S. Department of Commerce, Bureau of Census, 1961, Washington, D.C., p. 36. No information is given in this book for 1957. The figure for that year is extrapolated by using the 1956 figure and a growth rate of 1.3 per cent.

According to a sample survey of 228 agricultural cooperatives in 24 provinces in 1957 (*TCYC*, No. 8, 1958, pp. 8–12), an average of 3.7 man-days of unpaid labor were made by each person for "basic construction" within the cooperatives but excluding the labor drafted by the state. The imputed value of the unpaid labor is given as 2.6 yuan per person. Since the sample findings are suspected to be higher than the national averages, we scale down the imputed value of unpaid labor to 2 yuan per person. Therefore, the total imputed investment in the rural sector is put at 1,080 million yuan for 1957.

This per capita value is reasonable for the period of collectivization (1955–57), but it may be too high for the prior years, because, under a collective farming system, cooperative authorities would be inclined to use relatively more forced labor. According to another official survey report (*TCKTTH*, No. 8, 1955, p. 42), this type of unpaid labor in 1954 was only 75–83 per cent of 1957's rate. We use 80 per cent of 1957's rate and arrive at a value for imputed rural investment in 1954 of 864 million yuan.

We apply the 1957 level and the population indexes to obtain total imputed investments in 1955 and 1956, and use 1954's level and the population indexes to get corresponding figures for 1952 and 1953.

Table A-15
INTERNATIONAL COMPARISON OF THE STRUCTURE
OF FIXED INVESTMENT
(percentage)

Country	Share of construction	Share of producer durables
High-income countries		
Belgium	53	47
Canada	64	36
Sweden	62	38
United Kingdom	49	51
United States	63	37
Denmark	42	58
France	52	48
West Germany	47	53
Netherlands	50	50
Norway	47	53
Average	53	47
Medium-income countries		
Argentina	56	44
Austria	49	51
Chile	59	41
Ireland	57	43
Israel	70	30
Puerto Rico	68	32
Colombia	33	67
Greece	67	33
Panama	58	42
Union of South Africa	58	42
Average	58	42
Low-income countries		
Portugal	69	31
Ceylon	75	25
Taiwan	49	51
Ecuador	50	50
Ghana	64	36
Honduras	71	29
Peru	47	53

Table A-15 (Continued)

Country	Share of construction	Share of producer durables
Low-Income countries (*Continued*)		
Philippines	58	42
Burma	71	29
South Korea	70	30
Morocco	56	44
Nigeria	64	36
Average	62	38

SOURCES AND EXPLANATORY NOTES: The raw data are taken from S. Kuznets, "Quantitative Aspects of the Economic Growth of Nations," in *Economic Development and Cultural Change* 8, no. 4, pt. 2 (July 1960):80–83. They are national averages (arithmetic means) for the period 1951–57, at current prices. Kuznets originally grouped the countries in seven categories based on their per capita incomes in 1952–54. These countries are regouped here, however, as follows:

High-income countries   = Kuznets' (I) and (II)
Medium-income countries = Kuznets' (III) and (IV)
Low-income countries   = Kuznets' (V), (VI), and (VII)

For each group, the average shares are arithmetic means.

Table A-16

ADJUSTMENTS FOR LIU-YEH'S NATIONAL INCOME ESTIMATES, 1952–57
(in billions of 1952 yuan)

| | Gross Value of Food Crops | | | Construction | | | | |
	New estimates (1)	Liu-Yeh's estimates (2)	Difference between (1) and (2) (3)	New estimates (4)	Liu-Yeh's estimates (5)	Difference between (4) and (5) (6)	Liu-Yeh's estimates of GDP (7)	New estimates of GDP (8)
1952	20.33	21.63	−1.30	2.06	1.83	0.23	74.67	73.60
1953	20.78	22.09	−1.31	2.82	2.28	0.54	78.99	78.22
1954	21.49	22.82	−1.33	3.17	2.68	0.49	83.31	82.47
1955	22.23	22.97	−0.74	3.69	2.93	0.76	86.57	86.59
1956	23.02	22.82	0.20	5.60	4.97	0.63	97.28	98.11
1957	22.81	22.81	0	5.33	4.62	0.71	100.82	101.53

SOURCES: Columns (2), (5), and (7) are taken from T. C. Liu and K. C. Yeh, *The Economy of the Chinese Mainland*, pp. 66 and 397. Column (1) is derived by taking the Liu-Yeh estimate of gross value of grain production in 1957 and the grain output index given in Kang Chao, *Agricultural Production in Communist China*, Madison, 1970. Column (3) = (1) − (2). Column (4): figures for 1952–56 are taken from Kang Chao, *The Construction Industry in Communist China*, table 3, p. 69; the 1957 figure is extrapolated by using the 1956 amount and the rate of increase in construction labor force from 1956 to 1957 (see *ibid.*, table A-7, p. 202). Column (6) = (4) − (5). Column (8) = (7) + (3) + (6).

Abbreviations of Chinese
Periodicals and Books

CC   *Chien-chu* (Architecture).

CCCP   *Ching-chi chou-pao* (Economic Weekly).

CCCS   *Chien-chu chi shu* (Architectural Technique).

CCFH   Hsu Ti-hsin, *Chung-kuo-kuo-tu-shih-chi kuo-min ching-chi ti fen-hsi* (An Analysis of the National Economy during China's Transition Period). Revised ed. Peking: People's Publishing House, 1962.

CCHP   *Chien-chu hsueh-pao* (Journal of Architecture).

CCKJ   *Chien-chu kung-jen* (Construction Workers).

CCSC   *Chien-chu she-chi* (Architectural Design).

CCTC   *Chi-pen chien-she tung-chi-hsueh chiang-i* (Lectures on Basic Construction Statistics). SSB. Peking: Statistics Publishing House, 1956.

CCTLCS   *Chien-chu tsai-liao chi-shu* (Technique on Building Materials).

CCTLKY   *Chien-chu tsai-liao kung-yeh* (Building Material Industry).

CCYC   *Ching-chi yen-chiu* (Economic Research).

CH   State Statistics Bureau. *Wo-kuo kang-tieh tien-li mei-tan chi-hsieh fang-chih tsao-chih kung-yeh ti chin hsi* (The Present and Past Conditions of Our Iron and Steel, Power, Coal, Machinery, Textile and Paper Manufacturing Industries). Peking: Statistics Publishing House, 1958.

CHCC   *Chi-hua ching-chi* (Planned Economy).

CHKCSC   *Chi-hsieh kung-chang she chi* (Designing of Machine Building Plants).

CHKY   *Chi-hsieh kung-yeh* (Machinery Industry).
CHYTC   *Chi-hua yu tung-chi* (Planning and Statistics).
CKCNP   *Chung-kuo ching-nien pao* (China's Youth Daily).
CKHW   *Chung-kuo hsin-wen* (China News).
CKKJ   *Chung-kuo kung-jen* (Chinese Workers).
CKLY   *Chung-kuo lin-yeh* (China's Forestry).
CKNK   *Chung-kuo nung-ken* (China's Land Reclamation).
CKSL   *Chung-kuo shui-li* (China's Water Conservation).
CPCSWH   *Chi-pen chien-she wen-hsuan* (Selected Essays on Basic Construction). Peking: Basic Construction Publishing House. Various volumes.
CPJP   *Chin-pu jih-pao* (The Progress Daily).
CSCS   *Cheng-shih chien-she* (City Construction).
CSYK   *Chien-she yueh-kan* (Construction Monthly).
CYKC   *Chi-yeh kuai-chi* (Business Accounting).
EB   *Economic Bulletin*, Hong Kong.
FCKY   *Fang-chih kung yeh kuang-hui ti shih-nien* (Ten Glorious Years of the Textile Industry). Peking: Ministry of the Textile Industry, 1959.
FFYP   *First Five-Year Plan for Development of the National Economy of the People's Republic of China in 1954–1957.* Peking: Foreign Languages Press, 1956.
FKHP   *Chin-yung fa-kui hui-pien* (Collection of Financial Laws). Peking: Finance Publishing House. Various years.
HC   *Hung-chi* (Red Flag).
HCKTKY   *Chao-I-wen, Hsin-chung-kuo ti kung-yeh* (New China's Industry). Peking: Statistics Publishing House, 1957.
HCKTSL   *Hsin-chung-kuo ti shui-li chien-she* (New China's Water Conservation Construction). Peking: Finance and Economics Publishing House, 1956.
HCS   *Hsin-chien-she* (New Construction).
HH   *Hsueh-hsi* (Study).
HHKY   *Hua-hsueh kung-yeh* (Chemical Industry).
HHPYK   *Hsin-hua pan-yueh-kan* (New China Semimonthly).
HHYP   *Hsin-hua yueh-pao* (New China Monthly).
HKTKP   *Ta-kung pao*, Hong Kong.
HSYK   *Hsueh-shu yueh-kan* (Journal of Learning).
JMJP   *Jen-min jih-pao* (People's Daily).
JMST   *Jen-min shou-tse* (People's Handbook). Peking and Tientsin: Ta Kung Pao. Various years.
JMTT   *Jen-min tieh-tao* (People's Railways).
JMTY   *Jen-min tien-yeh* (People's Power Industry).

JPRS *U.S. Joint Publications Research Service.*

KCCS *Kung-cheng chien-she* (Engineering Construction).

KJJP *Kung-jen jih-pao* (Worker's Daily).

KL *Kung-lu* (Highway).

KMJP *Kuang-ming jih-pao* (Englightenment Daily).

KTSC Ko Chih-ta, *Kuo-tu-shih-chi ti wo-kuo yu-suan* (China's Budget in the Transition Period). Peking: Public Finance Publishing House, 1957.

KTTH *Kung-tso tung-hsun* (Bulletin of Activities).

KY *Kung-yeh chang-yung-ming-tsu-shu-yu chien-shih* (Concise Dictionary of Common Industrial Terminology). Peking: People's Publishing House, 1955.

KYTC *Kung-yeh-tung-chi kung-tso shou-tse* (Handbook of Industrial Statistical Work). Peking: Statistics Publishing House, 1956.

KYTCH *Kung-yeh tung-chi-hsueh* (Industrial Statistics). Wuhan: Hupei People's Publishing House, 1960.

LT *Lao-tung* (Labor).

LTTC *Lao-tung tung-chi kung-tso shou-tse* (Handbook of Labor Statistical Work). Peking: Statistics Publishing House, 1958.

MTCS *Chung-hua-jen-min-kung-ho-kuo fa-chan kuo-min-ching-chi ti i-ke wu-nien-chi-hua ti ming-tsu chien-shih* (Dictionary of the Terms in the First Five-Year Plan). Peking: People's Publishing House, 1955.

NK *Nan-kai chih-shu tzu-liao hui-pien* (Compilation of Nakai Index Materials). Peking: Statistics Publishing House, 1958.

PC *People's China.*

PR *Peking Review.*

SH *Shang-hai chieh-fand-chien-hou wu-chia-tzu-liao hui-pien 1921–1957* (Compendium of Data on Prices in Shang-hai before and after Liberation). Shanghai: Shanghai People's Publishing House, 1958.

SKJP *Hsin-chiang jih-pao* (Sinkiang Daily).

SLFT *Shui-li fa-tien* (Hydroelectricity).

SLHP *Shui-li hsueh-pao* (Journal of Water Conservation).

SLKYTH *Sen-lin kung-yeh tung-hsun* (Forest Industry Bulletin).

SLSTCS *Shui-li shui-tien chien-she* (Water Conservation and Hydroelectricity Construction).

SLYTL *Shui-li yu tien-li* (Water Conservation and Electric Power).

SN *San-nien-lai hsin-chung-kuo ti cheng-chiu* (New China's

Achievements in the Past Three Years). Peking: People's Publishing House, 1954.

SSB *State Statistical Bureau's Annual Communiqué on the Development of National Economy.*

SY *Shui-yun* (Waterway Transport.)

TC *Tsai-cheng* (Public Finance).

TCKT *Tung-chi kung-tso* (Statistical Work).

TCKTTH *Tung-chi kung-tso tung-hsun* (Statistical Work Bulletin).

TCYC *Tung-chi yen-chiu* (Statistical Research).

TGY *Ten Great Years: Statistics of the Economic and Cultural Achievements of the People's Republic of China.* Peking: Foreign Language Press, 1960.

TKP *Ta-kung pao* (Impartial Daily).

TL Niu Chung-huang, *Chung-kuo kung-yeh-hua ti tao-lu* (The Road of Industrialization in China). Peking: China Youth Publishing House, 1958.

TMKC *Tu-mu-kung-cheng* (Civil Engineering).

TMKCHP *Tu-mu-kung-cheng hsueh-pao* (Journal of Civil Engineering).

TSCYC *Tsai-ching yen-chiu* (Finance and Economic Research).

WKKM Niu Chung-huang, *Wo-kuo kuo-min-shou-ju ti chi-lei ho hsiao-fei* (Accumulation and Consumption in Our Country's National Income). Peking: China Youth Publishing House, 1957.

WKKY State Statistical Bureau, *Wo-kuo kung-yeh-tung-chi ti ching-yen* (Experiences Obtained from Our Country's Industrial Statistical Work). Peking: Statistics Publishing House, 1958.

WKT Niu Chung-huang, *Wo-kuo ti-i-ke wu-nien-chi-hua shih-chi ti sheng-tsan ho hsiao-fei kuang-hsi* (The Relationship between Production and Consumption in Our Country during the First Five-Year Plan Period). Peking: Finance and Economics Publishing House, 1959.

WKTCPCS Yun Chung, *Wo-kuo ti chi-pen-chien-she* (Our Country's Basic Construction). Peking: Workers Publishing House, 1956.

YCP *Yeh-chin pao* (Metallurgical Journal).

YSTE *Chien-chu-kung-cheng-yu-suai-ting-er* (Budgetary Norms of Civil Engineering). Peking: Civil Engineering Publishing House, 1958.

Bibliography

BOOKS AND ARTICLES IN ENGLISH

Aird, J. S. *The Size, Composition, and Growth of the Population of Mainland China*. Washington, D.C.: Bureau of Census, U.S. Department of Commerce, 1961.

Bergson, A. *The Real National Income of Soviet Russia Since 1929*. Cambridge: Harvard University Press, 1961.

Chao, Kang. *Agricultural Production in Communist China 1949–1965*. Madison: University of Wisconsin Press, 1970.

———. *The Construction Industry in Communist China*. Chicago: Aldine, 1968.

———. *The Rate and Pattern of Industrial Growth in Communist China*. Ann Arbor: University of Michigan Press, 1965.

———. "Pitfalls in the Use of China's Foreign Trade Statistics." *China Quarterly*, no. 19 (July–September, 1964):47–65.

———. *Estimation of Cultivated Area and Grain Output in Communist China, 1947–57*. Unpublished monograph.

Chen, Nai-ruenn. *Chinese Economic Statistics: A Handbook for Mainland China*. Chicago: Aldine, 1967.

Cheng, Chu-yuan, *The Machine-Building Industry in Mainland China*. Chicago: Aldine, 1972.

Cowan, C. D., ed. *The Economic Development of China and Japan*. London: Allen and Unwin, 1964.

Eckstein, A. *Communist China's Economic Growth and Foreign Trade*. New York: McGraw-Hill, 1966.

Eckstein, A., W. Galenson, and T. C. Liu, eds. *Economic Trends in Communist China*. Chicago: Aldine, 1968.

174

Ishikawa, S. *National Income and Capital Formation in Mainland China.* Tokyo: Institute of Asian Economic Affairs, 1965.

Klochko, M. A. *Soviet Scientist in Red China.* New York: Praeger, 1964.

Kuznets, S. *Commodity Flow and Capital Formation.* New York: National Bureau of Economic Research, 1938.

Li, C. M. *Economic Development of Communist China.* Berkeley and Los Angeles: University of California Press, 1959.

————, ed. *Industrial Development in Communist China.* New York: Praeger, 1964.

Liu, T. C., and K. C. Yeh. *The Economy of the Chinese Mainland: National Income and Economic Development, 1933–1959.* Princeton: Princeton University Press, 1965.

Moneta, C. "The Estimation of Transportation Costs in International Trade." *Journal of Political Economy,* 67, no. 1 (February 1959): 41–58.

Moorsteen, R., and R. P. Powell. *The Soviet Capital Stock, 1928–1962.* Homewood: Richard D. Irwin, 1966.

Rosovsky, H. *Capital Formation in Japan, 1868–1940.* Glencoe: Free Press, 1961.

Treadgold, D. W., ed. *Soviet and Chinese Communist: Similarities and Differences.* Seattle: University of Washington Press, 1967.

United Nations. *Economic Survey of Asia and the Far East.* Bangkok. Various years.

————. *The Growth of World Industry.* New York, 1963.

U.S., Congress, Joint Economic Committee. *An Economic Profile of Mainland China.* Washington, D.C., 1967.

Index